Today's Father

A GUIDE TO UNDERSTANDING, ENJOYING AND MAKING THINGS FOR THE GROWING FAMILY

Winston Press

Managing Editor   Susan Pinkus
Production Manager   David Alexander
Administration   Aline Davis, Sonia White

Contributors:
Dr. Michael Goldsmith
Jack Goodman
Professor Martin Herbert

Toy and furniture design by Mike Summers
and Gunter Ballati

Photography by Anthea Sieveking

The publishers also wish to thank Amanda, Annabel, Hannah,
Luke, Daniel, Michael, Nathaniel, Neil, Philippa, Rhiannon and
Richard for use of their drawings.

Winston Press, Inc.
430 Oak Grove, Minneapolis,
Minnesota 55403

Publishers' Note
Although our aim has been to provide a general guide from a
father's point of view to infant and child care, the advice contained
in **Today's Father** cannot embrace all circumstances, nor is it
intended as a substitute for consultation with a doctor. Serious
problems will, of course, require expert and sometimes prompt
medical care.

   Every care has been taken by the designers of the toys and
furniture featured to produce clear instructions for equipment that
is attractive, enjoyable to use and durable. However, it is essential
that, in making these items and in their use, the reader himself
takes all sensible safety precautions.

ISBN 0-86683-849-X
Library of Congress Catalog Card Number: 84-50002

Origination by East Anglian Engraving
Typeset by Spectrum
Printed in Great Britain by Cambus Litho, East Kilbride, Scotland

Today's Father

Contents

Foreword   5

The Concerned Father   7

The Weekend Father   35
   Family outings   36
   Shopping with children   37
   Out in the car   37
   Happy birthday!   38
   Safety first   42
   The absentee father   45
The Father Craftsman   47
   Tools and equipment   48
   Rocking cradle   51
   Chalkboard and easel   54
   Portable high chair   57
   Rocking horse   62
   Miniature wheelbarrow   66
   Building blocks   69
   Dollhouse   71
   Bird feeder   74
   Teddy bear book ends   77
   Desk with storage   79
   Hobby horse   82
   Pull-along snake   84
   Toy storage chest   86
   A perfect finish   91

Index   94

Further reading   95

Useful addresses   95

Foreword

Fathers are certainly taking a far greater interest than ever before in childbirth; of that there is no doubt. Many attend prenatal classes and are eager to be present at the birth. Yet doctors, teachers and psychologists alike report that later in childhood it is still primarily the mother who takes her child to doctor appointments or attends parents' meetings at school. This may, of course, to some extent be due to the restrictions sometimes inevitably posed by the world of work. But with so many mothers now in full- or part-time employment, it seems equitable that such duties should be shared. Ask any father how he feels about this, and the chances are that he will agree. What is more, you will probably find he has a whole host of questions about the physical and emotional development of the young family that he would like to ask of the professionals.

In **Today's Father,** a team of leading consultants looks at some of the most common paternal concerns, assuaging many unnecessary anxieties and providing excellent down-to-earth advice. Many ideas for weekend activities are included and a major section is devoted to designs and instructions for toys and furniture to make for children.

The publishers hope that their compendium for today's father will provide the basis for many informative and happy family hours.

The *Concerned* *Father*

Fathers, it seems, definitely want to know what
makes their children tick, and to be reassured they are
developing as healthily as possible. But there remains
an element of paternal reticence. For some reason,
fathers hesitate to show their interest actively. The
questions that follow cover some of the most common
areas of paternal concern, and have been collated as a
result of interviews with many hundreds of fathers.
Questions about behavior, sex education, schooling,
sibling rivalry and many other aspects of child
development feature.

Dr. Michael Goldsmith, a family doctor, Jack
Goodman, a lay psychotherapist, and Martin Herbert,
Professor of Psychology at Leicester University, offer
much food for thought in presenting their opinions.

Q What is the best way to take our two-year-old's temperature?

I am not convinced that you need to know your child's exact temperature all that often, as the signs of a fever are usually quite obvious. Using the back of your hand, where the temperature receptors are particularly efficient, against his or her forehead is a simple and effective method. Taking the temperature by mouth, as far as an infant is concerned, is definitely out. The rectal method is infinitely preferable. But a number of parents are not really confident about using a thermometer at all. So for them, the fever test strips that can be purchased in a pharmacy may provide the answer, even though they give a less accurate reading than a thermometer.

Sometimes, however, your child may have a raised temperature when there is nothing really wrong at all – perhaps because of overactivity or general excitement. But between the ages of eighteen months and two-and-a-half years, there can be a risk of febrile convulsions where the temperature reaches 102°F or more. In this instance, it will be essential to do all you can to cool the child down. Take off his or her clothes, lay the child on a towel in a warm place, and sponge with tepid water, without drying him or her off. The water will evaporate and cool the child down. Meanwhile, see that the doctor is called. Remember, too, that a very *low* temperature in a baby can also be dangerous, so be careful not to let a baby under six months of age get too cold, particularly at night. M.G.

Q Our son was adopted at six months old. He is now four. Do you think it wise to begin to tell him that he was adopted?

The fact that you are sensitive to your adopted child's needs reveals a lot about you as a parent. But then so does the fact that you have adopted a baby, because the authorities are always extremely careful about those with whom they place babies. It is very easy indeed, most people find, to become a parent the natural way; there are no 'qualifications' required as there are for the adoptive parent.

This realization should make you feel all the more secure in your role, and all the more confident about telling your child about his adoption because tell him you *must*. You know your child and therefore how much he can understand and accept at this tender age. Adoption may be explained in a number of ways. One successful approach is to bring up the matter when you see a small baby. Most parents, you might explain, have no choice in the baby they have, but you *chose* him. He was very special, and there was no one in the world who would love him quite as much as you. (There is no need to explain about infertility, even if this has relevance in your particular case). All your child needs to know at this stage is that he is wanted and always will be. He will then probably forget all about what you have told him for a while. It will have been a good idea to sow the seeds in his mind, however, so that he has an initial understanding of the situation; but whether you first do so at four, at five or at six is really a question of the maturity of the child.

The problem is greater when a child is adopted into an already existing family, and perhaps is also of a different race. Many adopting parents have successfully accomplished this by explaining that the family needed someone else to complete it and to make it whole, and that he was the right baby to join the family circle and share all the love it had to give.

Keeping adoption secret from a child until a late age – or, worse still, altogether – has been known to have drastic effects on the adoptive parent-child relationship and also the child's emotional stability. Get your child accustomed to the idea that he was adopted early on, and the chances are he will value your bond all the more when he begins to reach adulthood. It is quite a thought that one of the principal selling points of the highly successful Cabbage Patch dolls has been the adoption certificates with which they come.   J.G.

Q I sense that our eighteen-month-old daughter is becoming very attached to the woman who looks after her while my wife is at work. Is this something to be concerned about?

You are right to be thinking about the effect that such an attachment might have, for your daughter is quite likely to develop a particular fondness for and reliance on the person who spends the most time caring for her. What is more, those attachments we form early on in life are fundamental to the relationships we develop later. Scientific experiment seems to bear this out. Konrad Lorenz has shown that baby geese develop a lifelong attachment to any creature they see immediately after birth. Rhesus monkeys are found to cuddle up to artificial wire mothers in specific bonding experiments, too.

In this situation, it is quite natural for you to be asking yourself whether your wife has in some way abdicated her role as mother to a greater or lesser extent. Many fathers with working wives wonder whether this should be encouraged, whether they have made a mistake, and, if so, what they should do about it now.

But the answer is not a straightforward one because in certain circumstances it may in fact be preferable for another person to take on the day-to-day role of mother. Some women simply are not motherly, while some are better with children of an older age group. Some are utterly professionally committed, while some of course need to work for financial reasons. Who, therefore, does the busy working mother become in the child's eyes? This is a cause for great parental concern, and obviously something to be thrashed out sooner rather than later.

The working mother needs most essentially to spend as much time as possible with her child both first thing in the morning and last thing at night, and on weekends. At all costs, she must ensure that her child does not feel abandoned when she leaves for work. The child's attachment to a babysitter may well come to be resented by the mother, but the chances of this having a detrimental effect will be lessened if the problems are talked out. Far better for the child that there is continuity in a daycare situation than a constant change of people caring for her. Indeed, the repeated loss of those with whom a child forms attachments can have a devastating effect. The child discovers that the more people he or she comes to love, the more he or she gets hurt. Thus, as a protective mechanism in adult life, he or she may refuse both to love and be loved.

If a babysitter is reliable and shows affection for a child, the parents are fortunate. But any lingering doubts are certainly best brought into the open. The family of today certainly faces an enormous dilemma. So many fathers seem to be asking themselves if they really want a mother for their child, other than the one who bore the infant. But, as always, there is probably an answer to be found in compromise – perhaps by restricting working hours to enable a mother to see as much as possible of the child, perhaps by arranging to work at home, or perhaps by delaying the return to work for a while.   J.G.

Q **Our four-year-old always seems to be sick when we go out in the car. What can we do to prevent this?**

Many children seem to suffer from car sickness, so you are not alone in your problem. The important thing is to find out *why* your child is being sick, because there could be any one of a number of different causes. Most commonly, it is due to the actual motion of the car, almost as if the semicircular canals of the ears – responsible for balance – cannot "comprehend" that the vehicle is moving. The reason you and I are not usually sick is that we tend to look at things going on outside the car windows. Children, however, are most often playing with toys or reading in the car, and this in itself tends to bring on feelings of nausea. Encourage your child, therefore, to join in games that involve looking out of the window, and you should notice an improvement. It will also help to keep your child's mind from thinking about being sick, which in itself might bring it on.

Try, too, not to let the car get hot and stuffy, and to have plenty of fresh air.

A rare cause of car sickness is carbon-monoxide poisoning, which may be due to a leak in the exhaust pipe; it would be wise to check on this.

One other preventive measure sometimes adopted is to hang an antistatic chain or flap at the bottom of the car. It may be worth a try, but there is no definite scientific evidence to show that this actually works as far as car sickness is concerned.

Stopping the car journey for a break every hour or so and avoiding heavy meals may also help.

If all this fails, your doctor or pharmacist may perhaps recommend certain travel pills, suitable for children. Remember, though, that these may have the effect of making them feel drowsy.

Of course, if your child is prone to sickness, you will always be wise to take along a bag or bucket, tissues, and wet wipes, because it is not always possible to stop.   M.G.

Both parents have a role in giving sex education because *both* sexes are involved in the sexual act and in the loving attitudes that should surround it. Sex education is not only about sexual intercourse and biology but also about relationships, identity, and roles. What better way could there be for a boy or a girl to receive a rounded and realistic picture of the mysteries and joys of sex than from both parents, be it singly or together?

Some parents find it difficult to discuss these things, however. If this is the case, it is definitely best to do what you feel most comfortable with. Otherwise your child is likely to pick up inappropriate signals and feel that there is something embarrassing or tense-making about the subject of sex.

The very idea of trying to explain the facts of life in one special session is in itself quite erroneous. As they grow, all children show a healthy interest in their bodily functions, just as they are inquisitive about everything to do with the world they live in. This is a part of normal development, and all parents are bound to be asked questions about sex from time to time. "Where did I come from?" is a question commonly asked by four-year-olds, just as is "Why does the sun shine?" or "Why is the moon only there sometimes?" All such questions definitely merit a straightforward but brief explanation, rather than a detailed exposé. Too many facts will simply bore a child.

In order for them to grow up with well-balanced attitudes, children need to begin learning the facts of life from an early age. The facts should not be forced upon them, however. Nor should sex education be a matter of merely factual instruction about puberty, menstruation, intercourse, and reproduction. It has a far wider meaning than widely attributed to it, with values, moral attitudes, and relationships all importantly coming into play.

Unfortunately, a parent will frequently try to fob off a child's questions by referring him or her to the other parent. But sex education is essentially a joint responsibility, even though it may perhaps be the case that matters of male or female hygiene are best explained by a parent of the same sex. By hearing about the facts of life gradually and from both parents, a child should more readily come to appreciate that love and sex are ideally based on mutual male-female respect and understanding.

It has been said that when a child asks about reproduction, that is the time to answer him or her. But what if the child *never* makes the opening gambit by asking a question? It may be wise to preempt by taking advantage of an event such as a marriage or birth in the family, using it as a casual starting-point for a preliminary chat. If, however, a child cannot open up in order to ask questions, it may be something in parental attitudes that hinders his or her approach. If your children discover that you can speak freely they will become less fearful of their curiosity

Q Do you think that both parents should be involved with explaining the facts of life to children of either sex?

and give voice to their questions, thoughts, and feelings. Behavior as well as questions may also indicate whether your children have some sort of curiosity bottled up inside.

Remember, too, that information about sex – whatever the words used – should always be given in the simplest possible terms. Sadly, there is a tendency for people to become verbose and euphemistic when talking to children about sex.

Many teenagers feel too shy and prickly to approach their parents about sexual problems and anxieties, and this is where sex education at school can be particularly helpful. Concerns may be quite bizarre, but nonetheless intensely felt for all their unreasonableness. Even in these enlightened days, as we like to think of them, there are still young girls who believe that they can become pregnant because a boy kisses them, and boys who think they will go mad or become blind because they masturbate.

But the most important aspect of sex education in its broadest aspect is the example set for children by their parents. Through the kind of family life they have, they can learn that love and sex are based on respect for other human beings, a respect that they will only feel for others if they have it for themselves.

Always try to answer any of your child's questions truthfully and in a clear fashion. Difficulties are bound to arise when sex education is treated as something to be discussed in hushed tones, if at all.

In this area, as in many others, George Bernard Shaw's maxim applies. *The only golden rule is that there are no golden rules.* In other words, there is no timing and technique that can be applied rigidly to all children and all parents. Children vary, family situations differ. This means that only guidelines can be suggested, and even these must be interpreted with flexibility. There are many so-called experts on sex education and many books on the subject, but the views they express often differ and are, in the end, opinions, even though very often informed opinions, based on experience.

Your child's school may provide formal sex education at various stages, but as with so many aspects of life, it is within a good home environment that example is best set and guidance given.   M.H.

Q **How do you think we should best explain to our three-year-old that his grandpa has just died? They loved each other's company and spent a great deal of time together.**

It is hard for an adult to come to terms with bereavement, but in some ways it is a little easier for a child to accept the fact that he will not see his grandfather again. Put the situation to a child, and he will accept it as a fact of life. Only as we grow up does it become more difficult.

A simple, straightforward explanation should suffice, providing you speak calmly about what has happened. It's best for a child not to see his parents overwrought. Explain that his grandfather was ill, that he was old, and that he died, which is something that happens to everyone when they get very old.

Explain, too, that this means that he will not see him any more, and that he will probably miss his grandpa, just as you will. But just because he is dead, that doesn't mean that his grandpa will be forgotten. Mention, too, how fortunate he is to have had a grandpa who loved him so much and who spent so much time with him. Tell him this as succinctly as you can. The chances are that, at age three, he will react by being both upset and curious at first, but then get on with his day.

Opinions vary as to whether a child should be present at a funeral. On the whole, for a toddler, it would probably be a frightening experience to witness either the disappearing coffin or the burial. But there is no reason at all for him not to visit the cemetery once the headstone has been set. Most psychologists would probably agree that respect for the memory of previous generations is an excellent quality to instil in a child.   J.G.

Q We had promised our ten-year-old a special present if he did well in his school exams, but he did not, even though I think he tried very hard. Should we still buy him the computer game he wanted so much?

You have a problem here because you promised to reward him for results rather than effort, and also because it's a good rule generally to stick to your word, so that you don't debase the currency. I would give him a small consolation prize for trying, but in the future think through fairly precisely what the incentive is for, and how the attainment of a particular goal can be agreed upon, so that there are no ambiguities about whether the child has reached the objective or not.

From very early in a child's life, effort and application are stressed and rewarded as positive values, and idleness is regarded as a negative quality. The confusing thing about achievement for the perceptive child is the lack of an obvious connection between ends and means. Indoctrination with the virtues of work sometimes makes it seem that the mere activity of working is an end in itself, whatever the nature of the work.

Parents become particularly concerned when a child falls short of standards that are expected, and when he performs significantly below the level they would predict in terms of his general ability. Certainly, the home environment and parental encouragement are most potent factors in determining the child's achievement at school, just as is good teaching and an imaginative curriculum. The educational aspirations of parents for their child, the literacy of the home, and the interest of the parents in the child's work all influence the level of the child's achievements. If parents are not encouraging or are overdemanding, if they nag and are destructive in their criticism, the child will be demoralized or become overanxious. Why should he work hard when all his efforts, good and bad, are condemned? His confidence will be destroyed, and he may retreat behind a mask of stupidity and "don't care" laziness. Or he may be so concerned that he starts to panic.

Some children repeatedly perform poorly when tested principally because of nervousness in a stress situation. A meeting with your child's teacher will probably help put the whole thing into perspective. Bear in mind that children, too, are usually disappointed by poor results, not only parents.

To some youngsters, failure acts as an incentive to try harder. To others, it merely confirms an existing conclusion and they throw in the sponge. It is this matter of your child's expectations of success or failure that is important to his performance. Each child has his own subjective expectations of future achievements and the main factor that determines how he rates himself – for example, with exam performances – is his past performance.

If he has done well in the past, he will expect to do well in the future. A series of achievements will set up in his mind what we call "subjective hypotheses" – theories about his own accomplishments and potential – that he will use to predict his own performance. Each subsequent performance will add to what he already knows about a particular activity, and may modify his ideas about the probability of success at it. If the child has been repeatedly successful in a particular endeavor, it is likely that he will acquire a general expectation of success, and each performance of the activity will be accompanied by rising expectations. Success may also result in an increased liking for the activity, and an increased motivation to succeed. As they say, nothing succeeds like success.

The effects of feelings of failure are more variable than those of success. If a child does not achieve what he has expected to achieve but accepts his failure in a realistic manner, he will lower his expectations for the next performance. Sometimes, however, a child will react to failure by raising his expectations. He may simply blame his failure on some external obstacle. The expectations of people important to the child also play a part in how he reacts to failure. If there is pressure on him, he may continue to base his expectations at a level far above what is realistic.

Sadly, there are some children who are unable to attain their own goals, or the goals of their parents, because they are dominated by fear of failure, and therefore avoid at all costs any situations involving stress, achievements, and competition.

Have you set expectations that are too high? Are you pressurizing your child by offering rewards for standards that are hard to achieve? The effectiveness of a reward depends partly on the child's expectation of success in a particular undertaking. If he has a low expectation of passing an arithmetic test, for example, yet is successful, the value of any reward occasioned by the triumph will be far greater than if he expected to succeed.

On the other hand, gentle criticism of failure may serve as an incentive for the basically bright and able child, who may double his efforts to avoid encountering such a situation again. The constantly failing child *expects* failure and criticism, hence it has little effect on him, except to confirm his worst beliefs. But an experience of praise or reward is so striking and so sweet that he works twice as hard to encounter this state of affairs again.

All of this goes to say that we need to think very carefully about rewards and criticisms in trying to get the best out of our children. Determined effort, even if it results in only minimal achievement, merits praise. A tangible reward may then be given for greater achievement. M.H.

Q For unavoidable reasons, we are having to send our seven-year-old son to boarding school. How should we best prepare him for this?

The most important thing that you will need to convey to a child in this situation is that a boarding school education is not tantamount to a rejection. But go back a step for a moment. A child of seven can in no way be protected from anxieties that exist within the home. If, as you say, the reasons for sending your son to boarding school are unavoidable, the implication is that, if circumstances were different, your son would remain at home. It is therefore quite likely that, in the process of this decision-making, there has been tension in the domestic air, and your son may have picked this up. *How* to tell your child is thus somewhat secondary to the consideration that your child will already have sensed that something is up. You will have to tread gently.

Your child may experience the news that he is to be away from home during the school year as something of a shock, even though he is already aware that something is afoot; so a prime concern must be how to reduce that shock to a minimum. Your child is going to feel a sense of bereavement at leaving home – just as you will at his leaving. But the parental burden should not be placed upon the child.

The best approach to the problem is not perhaps the most obvious one. Let your child think that it is an excellent idea for him to be going to boarding school and the odds are he will feel you are anxious to get rid of him. At seven, he will probably be sufficiently advanced to accommodate the circumstances, so explain to him precisely why you have had to make this choice about his education. Then you can begin to point out some of the benefits of boarding school life, and explain about visits and holiday arrangements.

If you are considering sending him away for a few days – to a relative or friends, perhaps – so that he has some experience of coping with a different environment before he starts boarding school, my advice to you would be to forget the idea. Perhaps the visit will prove to be a disaster. What then? It could be that as a result of any such unhappy "rehearsal", he will become entrenched in a desire not to leave home, and therefore he will be starting the new experience of boarding school in a negative frame of mind.

It is an excellent idea, however, to visit the school together in advance, so that your son starts off with a

picture of what to expect by way of the building and its layout. It is important to maintain regular contact during the school year, but beware of the temptation to write every other day if this is not something you will be able to maintain in a regular fashion. Encourage your son to take along with him any possessions that make him feel comfortable but not those that may make him seem a baby in the eyes of the other boys. Check on the policy of the school and on the sort of belongings pupils of his age tend to bring. Remember, too, that a long goodby can be embarrassing to a seven-year-old and emotionally exhausting for everyone. Your son will probably show you himself when he is ready to be left. It is bound to be a difficult time, but since you have no other option, check carefully on the school's reputation and start planning how you will spend the holidays together.

J.G.

Q **Our four-year-old seems to love playing with his older sister's dolls. Is this anything to be concerned about? He shows no interest at all in more traditionally masculine toys.**

The initial response to such a question must be to ask whether a child has sufficient toys of his own. Is there a choice of toys available to him? Has he any very "masculine" toys? Have you encouraged his play by joining in with games of the more "masculine" kind? It may be that because he has an older sister, he is imitating her pattern of play. Many boys these days actually play with dolls, although neither they nor their parents may think of it in that way. Look at the popularity of toy soldiers and robots.

Gender is imposed on each individual from the moment fertilization takes place, when a particular combination of chromosomes determines the sex of the embryo; but although physical gender is decided at conception, it takes several weeks of embryonic life before the first slight signs of sexual differentiation are manifested.

What evidence we have suggests that, from the psychological point of view, the newborn human is not in any essential sense sexually differentiated. Gender identity is acquired during childhood; from as early as the second year in life, the child begins to distinguish between masculine and feminine. By four years of age, he or she has divided the world into male and female people, and is preoccupied with boy-girl distinctions. The debate continues as to whether we should lessen these distinctions and bring up our children so as not to make strong differences between the male and female roles. But it certainly seems that, even in those families in which parents have attempted to play down differences, preference for one sex role or the other begins to emerge quite early in life, most usually by the third or fourth year. By the age of seven, a child is strongly committed to shaping his or her behavior to his or her biological sex, and he or she will usually show anxiety and even anger when accused of acting in those ways that are traditionally regarded by society as being characteristic of the behavior of the opposite sex.

Sexual patterns of behavior – such as identification with a particular gender, sexual arousal, and styles of sexual gratification – are very complex; hormonal, environmental, cultural, and social factors all play a part in determining them.

A fondness for playing with dolls is often an area of concern to parents who are very bound up with traditional roles or where (in a single-parent situation) a mother is anxious about the effect of the absence of an adult male figure in the home. Such worries come to a head if a male child shows a very strong preference for girls' pursuits.

In our society, girls are allowed more leeway to pattern themselves on aspects of the male sex role. They may wear skirts or trousers, for instance. But imagine the reaction to a boy in a dress! It is also culturally acceptable for girls to have masculinized names, and to play with boys' toys. Because of the inflexibility of the masculine role, boys are usually more aware of sex-appropriate behavior than girls. This is why it might be of concern if seemingly inappropriate behavior and choices continue for a long time and if, as a boy gets older, he is exclusively interested in feminine things. But it is in no way unusual for a four-year-old boy or girl to get fun out of creative play that may involve dolls. Such preference at this stage is probably of little importance, but you may like to check that the toy chest actually offers some choice of playthings, not exclusively dolls. M.H.

Q **Do you think it is a good idea for children to learn to swim as babies?**

While children are sometimes nervous of the water, babies usually take to swimming very easily. So I do think it an excellent idea for children to learn to swim as young as possible. They do, however, need to be in the care of someone who knows how to handle a baby in the water, and this is not something that a parent does particularly well by instinct. If a baby is healthy, he or she can start to learn from three months onwards. It is, of course, vital not to let a very small baby get too cold. A temperature-controlled pool is best unless you live in a very warm climate. M.G.

Q **I recently found some dreadful comics hidden in our nine-year-old child's room. How can we stop him reading this sort of thing?**

The essence of the problem is that children quite often like reading something that their parents do not approve of, so one has to ask whether it is in fact right to make a value judgment for a nine-year-old. What is more, if a child feels he has to read his comics in secret, this could be a sign that there is an element of breakdown in communication within the family. It may be that he has come to relish these comics because of the very fact that he knows that there is something about them that mom and dad don't like.

Children like being scared on the whole. That accounts for the popularity of certain children's serials on television as well as many spooky movies. But the chances are that the comics today's children are reading are not actually as terrifying as the stories we were weaned on. Take another look at Grimm's Fairy Tales. In many ways stories about wicked stepmothers and witches who carry off young children are much more frightening.

The important thing is to see that a child is encouraged to read as widely as possible. Sometimes a child turns to comics because there is simply not enough other stimulating reading matter in the home. It is a good idea to take your child to the library as often as possible and perhaps to join a special children's book club. Make suggestions to him by way of recommended books, but do not force him to read what does not seem to interest him. As with all things, it is a matter of balance. Remember, too, to encourage a child to look up in an encyclopedia any facts he wishes to find out about. That is an important skill to be mastered, and will stand him in good stead. Meanwhile, if he wants to regress to comics every now and then, why not let him? What is wrong with children being children? When you come to think about it, they are going to be adults for so long.   J.G.

Q **Our daughter is almost four and absolutely terrified of the dark. What is the best way to help her through this?**

If a child is really terrified of the dark, rather than being merely fearful, she may have a phobia – an excessive fear that goes well beyond the developmental fears that most children of four or five years of age have about the dark.

There could be many reasons why her fear has become so extreme. Was she ever put in a dark room as a punishment? Did she perhaps spend a lot of time in your room when younger, and is not yet used to being in a bedroom of her own? Or is this a new bedroom and she is still not quite familiar with her surroundings?

On the other hand, she may have heard about ghosts or wild animals, and the dark may be incidental to the real fear.

The best thing to do is to try gently to "tease out" what it is that really worries her when she is in the dark and alone. The tendency of a child to overreact with fear is closely related to the inherited sensitivity of her nervous system and very early influences, even those going back to the child's first environment – the mother's womb. It has been suggested that if the mother is under considerable stress during pregnancy, this may make her child more jumpy and more highly strung than she might otherwise be.

In this sort of situation, a parent will do well to think back. A child's fear of the dark might be due to something that has happened in the past. Occasionally, experiences of a very frightening kind can condition a child to feel acute apprehension in similar situations later, and this conditioning can persist. Was there ever an incident, for instance, when it was thought a burglar was trying to make an entrance? Or was there any other alarm that might have had a similar effect?

All children – and especially those who start life by

being naturally prone to anxiety – are very susceptible to the contagious effects of the emotions their parents express. They are adept at picking up even the smallest signs that betray their parents' feelings, so many youngsters actually learn to fear the dark.

To be left in the dark is not initially an unpleasant experience for a child. Sooner or later, however, when she is in pain with a stomachache, frightened by a dream, hungry, cold, or miserably wet, she will cry for her mother or father. When they come to her aid, they inevitably put on the light as they enter the room to console her. What better conditioning model could there be for associating darkness with distress, and light with a kind of reward in the form of a comforting mother or father! Try entering the room without putting on the light. Chat to your child and reassure her until the trouble has been identified, only then switching on the light to remedy the situation. This sequence of events ensures that there is no direct and recurrent relationship between the presence of the parent and the light.

Remember, too, that punishment is quite inappropriate. You cannot bully a child out of fear, although you may succeed in punishing him or her into submission so that the child learns to be secretive about the terror. The price of this, of course, is loss of confidence in you, as well as the possibility of new symptoms appearing in addition to the suppressed fear.

An alternative approach would be to acknowledge that your child has acquired a terror of the dark that is perfectly genuine and to attempt to reshape her behavior along the lines that you wish to encourage, making use of what psychologists call "positive reinforcements". For example, you might leave on a bedside light, switching it off when your child is sleeping. But leave the door ajar with a light on in the hall so that she will not be in total darkness if she awakes. To avoid sudden distress, make sure that she knows how to switch on the light should she wake up and want it on. Because the situation is now under the child's control, there will be no call for a panic reaction.

Above all, never let the situation become a contest of wills. Once this happens, you will have defeated your original purpose of enlisting your child's own energies in coping with the problem. M.H.

Gentle persuasion, I feel, is the ideal solution. Try as hard as you can not to make a big thing about it. Your daughter will have a lot to cope with in getting used to her new school environment, so that the additional stress of taking away from her what is possibly a very important psychological prop may prove too much. The chances are that she will kick the habit of her own accord, anyway. If you let her take her favorite blanket or soft toy to school, this may help. M.G.

Q Our four-year-old will soon be starting school and is still sucking her thumb. What can we do about this?

Q Why does the middle child always seem to have such a hard time of things? How can we best avoid this happening in our family?

The first child is usually aware of his or her place in the family and takes on responsibility for any younger ones. The youngest one, meanwhile, is always the baby. It is the middle child who mostly gets the short end of the stick. Although there are exceptions, research has shown that it is comparatively rare for a middle child to reach great heights in a career.

In order to maximize a middle child's potential, it is essential to remember at all times not to overlook his or her needs, to treat him or her very much as an individual, and to develop to the full those areas in which he or she shows most skills. The only alternative may be to alter his or her position in the hierarchy by adding to the family. Three is often a difficult number.   J.G.

Q Some of the tales I have found in books of so-called fairy stories seem positively horrific, yet our children love them. Could they be harmful in any way?

These stories may be horrific to you; but if your children are enjoying them, it is unlikely that they are really harmful. Children enjoy excitement and, when actually safe, love being frightened out of their wits. They savor the mysteries and horrors of the unknown and the supernatural, and by experiencing terrifying things vicariously, they come to terms with some of life's problems and unpleasantness. It is in many ways practice at anxiety-management. So let the adrenaline surge through their systems; it is all part of the learning process.

The time to intervene and call a halt is when there is a more vulnerable, hypersensitive child who begins to have bad dreams or who is frightened to go to bed. Perhaps the stories that upset children most are those that involve separation of children from their parents, stories about children who are lost or become orphans. In the end, it is a matter for judgment. But if a child asks for more, there is probably no harm at all in the stories you are reading. He or she will soon let you know if the story lines are too terrifying.

It is helpful to remember that childhood is a period of vivid imagination, fantasy, make-believe, and magic; to the imaginative preschool child, what his parents sometimes think is outlandish is often not quite so strange. The borderline between fact and fantasy is not yet clearly defined, and what a child has wished or dreamed may sometimes seem more real than mere fact. Preschool children may even imagine that they can influence events by magical application of their will. Indeed, between twenty and fifty percent of children are thought to have imaginary playmates who may seem as vivid and substantial to them as real people. Most of such invisible companions have vanished, however, by the time the child is eight or nine. There is nothing reprehensible about such made-up things. Children even use fantasy as a means of explaining relationships and situations about which they feel unsure.

Much concern is also often expressed as to whether children can actually learn to be violent as a result of terrifying stories. In the old days, it was the "penny horribles" that were widely blamed, then it was movies and today it is largely television. There is little or no evidence of an objective kind that can supply a complete answer to this question. Certainly, on the average, children spend a good deal more time watching their parents than watching television. Children imitate, so it may lie mostly in the parental court to supply a nonviolent model. What children make of violent stories is also determined to a large extent by what their parents teach them to make of it.

Try questioning your child and discussing the stories you read to him. This will soon establish the true situation.   M.H.

Children do tend to tailor their behavior to the particular places and particular people in and with whom they find themselves, and this chameleon capacity often leads to misunderstandings between home and school. A child tends to look around him, consider the rules that apply in that situation, how other children behave, and what is expected of him. Then he adapts his behavior accordingly. This is what in psychological jargon is known as "situation specificity". We know that children who show problems at home very seldom do so at school, and those who show problems at school quite often do not show problems at home. However, a teacher may be convinced that home conditions are causing bad behavior at school, and this can quite understandably cause tremendous embarrassment at times.

It is easy to forget just how radical is the adjustment required when starting school. For the majority of children, going to a preschool or a daycare center is the first experience of separation from home. For fairly long periods each weekday, or on certain weekdays, your child is removed from familiar, comfortable routines with a nurturing parent nearby and has to face the hurly-burly of preschool or daycare life. The mantle of authority has been handed over to strangers, and the child has been moved from what is a predictable environment, where his or her requirements are well understood, to one where, at least for a few weeks, life is full of the unexpected, and sometimes the unpleasant. The demands and stresses of the new situation, real or imaginary, are many. A child requires a good deal of flexibility and self-control to cope with them.

Don't forget, either, that for the first time those apparently trivial but, to the sensitive child, extremely intimate functions – such as washing, eating, and going to the toilet – have to be carried out with less privacy. The child has also to learn about getting along with children who have a point of view of their own, and who may not always take others' feelings into account.

At times, too, troubles may arise because parents and teachers do not see eye to eye about discipline and rules. It is helpful if you can discuss these matters

Q In talking about Robert's progress with his preschool teacher, we seemed to be discussing a different child. He is a model child at home, but apparently very naughty at school. Is this a common phenomenon?

with the teacher in order to reach agreement about the management of any undesirable behavior. It may be that if Robert is a "model" child at home, you are overdoing things on the discipline front. Children can be *too* good. At this age, one would *expect* children to be a little difficult, as they test out their individuality on those in authority.

If it is fear that we are talking about, then it would be an excellent idea for either parent to spend a little time with the child at the preschool before leaving him there. With sensitive and sensible handling, these difficulties should soon be overcome.   M.H.

Q **How can we put a stop to the very obvious competition that exists between our seven- and eight-year-old daughters?**

An element of sibling rivalry is perfectly normal and very healthy. Indeed, the danger may lie in suppressing it because, in doing so, you will probably be suppressing not only a child's very personality but also his or her ambitions. While children may come from the same home and the same parents, they are essentially individuals who will grow up to lead different lives. Would you rather have sired a set of clones?

Rivalry of this kind is usually accentuated where there is very little age difference. Parents faced with this kind of problem need to ask themselves whether the children are being treated in a fair and unbiased manner.

If you have two children and one is short-sighted, they will not both need spectacles. Parents should do all they can to treat each member of the family according to individual needs and abilities. It is often the attempt to stamp each of them out of the same mould that brings about acute sibling rivalry.   J.G.

Q **Our baby seems very slow to speak. Could there be something wrong?**

There are three principal approaches to the matter of slowness to speak. First of all, a child may simply be a slow developer in this particular area – quite normal or even advanced in other respects but tardy in talking. Some children may have started to walk "on time" but lag behind when it comes to communicating. Given time, however, they will probably catch up.

Other children are slow to talk because they find no real *need* to speak. Their parents speak *for* them. How often have you heard a mother or father use such phraseology as "Would baby like a cookie?" rather than encouraging the child to ask for one! It is important to *motivate* a child to speak. Why, after all, should children bother to be articulate when they can get what they want simply by grunting?

Occasionally, however, there can be more of a problem when a child will not talk. Slow speech may, for instance, be due to hearing difficulties, to emotional disturbance, or to general retardation. What I would say is that if you have tried to give your child time, made every effort to communicate, and there is still no sign of improvement, expert professional help may be called for. He or she will, of course, also be looking at your child's development as a whole. Bear in mind that no two children develop at exactly the same rate. So you need not be perturbed if one of your children is a little slower to speak than another. Each child is an individual, developing at his or her own particular pace. Girls are sometimes thought to be a little quicker to speak than boys, but there does not seem to be a very significant difference. I would also add that you should not expect too much of your child. Don't be upset if he or she is not word-perfect. Every toddler has special words for things. This in itself does not matter. But if you *always* speak to your child in baby talk, then that will, of course, be all he or she will learn. M.G.

Q **How important do you think the presence of father figure really is?**

There have been many studies about the effects of a motherless childhood but few about paternal absence. However, it seems clear that life can often become complex for a child who is brought up with no father figure at all and in an entirely female environment. A daughter, too, may find it difficult to adjust to womanhood if there has been no father figure. Not all children are fortunate enough to have their real fathers around, but this does not mean that they need necessarily be deprived because an uncle, a grandparent, a family friend, or some other adult male may take on the role of father figure quite effectively.

In childhood, we all need a constant and reliable father figure offering a model of the male's role in society and a template of the male-female relationship. In later life, our behavior continues to be influenced by those with whom, as children, we identify and whose example we emulate. J.G.

Q **What is the right age to start giving a child spending money?**

By all means, open a savings account in the name of your child when he or she is born and put something aside on a regular basis. But actually giving a child pocket money involves several learning processes and, as such, it is probably unwise to give children money of their own before they understand first of all what it is, something about its possible uses (because this can involve something other than spending), and also the concepts of cheaper and more expensive, better and worse.

In an attempt to illustrate to our son the range of possibilities, from the time he was three years old, we let him have a coin of a very small denomination every time he left home. Without fail, the use to which he chose to put it was a poor box. In fact, many a time he refused to go home until he had found one.

As for the older child, try to come to a clear understanding as to what you expect him or her to buy out of pocket money, and what you will provide. You may also find that you are going to have to be strong if the going rate among your child's contemporaries is higher than either you can afford or you think is a suitable level. Having spending money of their own will certainly help children develop a sense of values. In fact, posssibly the only way to help make children responsible as far as money is concerned is to give them a little more than they need. They may be tempted to squander it at first, but it could present an excellent opportunity for you to show them some of the possible options as far as investment – even on a very modest scale – is concerned. J.G.

Q **Would you recommend that our newborn baby be vaccinated against whooping cough?**

It is now quite definitely safer to have the vaccination for whooping cough than not to be immunized against it at all. In the first year of life, an attack of whooping cough can be very serious and the experience of seeing the suffering a child goes through is sufficient to make any parent wish his or her baby *had* been vaccinated against it. The number of children who have been vaccine-damaged has been greatly exaggerated in reports. There is in fact considerably less risk of damage as a result of vaccination than there is from actually contracting the disease. Before the vaccination is given, however, you will be asked to confirm whether there is any history of seizures in the family or certain allergies because, in some rare instances, the vaccination against whooping cough may indeed be inadvisable. M.G.

Q **Do you consider that the only child is in any way disadvantaged?**

It is often assumed that the only child is, by virtue of the fact that he or she is the parents' sole offspring, inevitably spoilt. In reality, however, the only child widely *lacks* certain benefits that the child from a more extensive family acquires quite naturally.

The parents of the only child will almost certainly have more time. They will be able to hand on more tangible assets, too. What their son or daughter will inevitably miss out on, however, is the opportunity to learn how to live and share with siblings and to respect their needs. It is also usually the case that he or she will spend far more time in adult company and thus mature more rapidly. There are, as you see, both advantages and disadvantages to being an only child, so that what is lost on the swings – if you are careful to keep a balanced attitude – can be gained on the merry-go-rounds. J.G.

Q **I am always nervous that our son might choke on candy or a bone. If this ever happened, what would be the best procedure?**

The most straightforward way to get a child to cough up something in his throat is to put him over your knee and to give a good, sharp thump between the shoulder blades. If this fails, then holding the child upside down and thumping him on the back is the next best thing. If that doesn't work, then the Heimlich maneuvre may be called for. This involves pressing the child's solar plexus from behind, forcing a lot of pressure into the chest and thus ejecting the foreign body. Classes to learn this procedure are offered by the Red Cross and other agencies giving instruction in first aid.

If a fish bone or any other foreign body stuck in the throat refuses to budge, it is best to talk to your doctor right away. He or she will advise you what to do. If your child is actually choking, call an ambulance or rush your child to the emergency room of the nearest hospital.

There are, of course, certain things you can do in the attempt to prevent this ever happening. Carefully cut hot dogs into small pieces. Try to remove all bones from any fish served, and avoid giving young children hard candy, peanuts, popcorn or chewing gum. M.G.

Q **Would you recommend that I take paternity leave when our next baby is born?**

In spite of tremendous advances in attitudes towards childbirth, it is still not widely recognized that – psychologically, if not physically – the concerned father goes through a pregnancy, too. Indeed, as if in emphasis of this basic fact, in certain so-called primitive tribes, the woman bears the child and the father acts out the birth process!

Parenthood, however many times it happens, is always a new experience. Although those having a second or subsequent child may think that the event will not be quite so exciting the next time around, it always proves to be a time of great emotion. On a practical level, it is helpful if the father can be around to help with domestic chores during the first couple of weeks or so. His presence at home will, of course, also be very reassuring to any other child in the family who otherwise might feel that his mother has abandoned him or her in favor of the new baby. Such paternal concern bodes well for the future of the newly enlarged family, and throughout the western world, paternity leave is now commonly granted. J.G.

Q **Do you think it advisable for our teenage daughter to take a vacation job?**

Providing your daughter is enthusiastic about the prospect of working, there is probably no harm in this at all. On the other hand, if this is something you are imposing against her will, it would definitely be inadvisable. Allow her to develop a resentful attitude towards work at this stage, and it could affect her whole working life. The consequences of thrusting a job upon her before she is either emotionally willing or eager – particularly if it is not a job of her choice – could be disastrous. The risk is that work might easily become associated with something she definitely does not want to do.

If the idea has come from her in the first place, however, why not let her prove herself? You will of course, need to check up on the legalities as far as her age is concerned.

Working experience will enable her to meet people in a environment other than home and school, and finding that she has to work so many hours in order to earn enough for a pair of shoes or some other item will provide a picture of the real world and how hard her parents have to work for what they want out of life.

Do let her have some free time during the summer vacation, though. For many of us, our school years are the last time we ever have several weeks off at a stretch.   J.G.

Q **How would you suggest I cope with dumb insolence?**

This is a situation that many parents seem to encounter, and I am not surprised if you find your child's behavior utterly infuriating if only because, in many ways, he is issuing through his silent ploy something of a direct challenge. A common behavior pattern in pre- or early adolescence – that is, from about nine years of age onwards – it is more frequent in boys than in girls, probably because the young males of our species go through a period involving more of an identity crisis than do girls.

Until now, your child has probably identified most of all with his mother. He has cuddled up to her for comfort, cried for her when upset, looked to her for encouragement. Now, however, as he grows towards manhood, he feels the need to identify more with the father figure and so may find himself straddling two worlds. His dumb insolence is at one and the same time both an enormous plea by the child in him for help and attention, and a first attempt by the adolescent in him at rebellion against parental authority.

Children both love and hate their parents, and experience a whole range of other emotions towards them, too. They may loathe them, adore them, despise them, and worship them – and may even feel all these responses towards them simultaneously. What they never are, however, is indifferent toward their parents.

What a child finds very hard to accept, therefore, is parental indifference. In fact, he needs a constant demonstration of parental involvement, even if this means a display of certain negative feelings at times. It is quite normal for a child to prefer to be scolded than to be ignored. So, you see, dumb insolence is often quite simply a plea for attention. Have you been doing enough to show your child the extent of your interest in his world? Have you spent much time with him lately? When was the last time you had a good, long chat? Ask yourself these questions. You may find that the dumb insolence you are meeting with is actually a silent language with a vocabulary all its own, one in which the principal phraseology seems to be "Stop ignoring me! Don't take me for granted! You seem to notice me only when I do something wrong."

How often do you praise your child when he is doing well? Do most of your communications take place when he has been at fault? Sadly, this is so often the case with fathers and children in today's busy world. If your child finds the only way he can elicit a response from you is by misbehaving, then he will continue to use this route as the result of what will

have become a sort of conditioning process. In this type of situation, you have to break the circle. You have no other option, or communication between you may break down altogether.   J.G.

It is perfectly normal for her to want to experiment in this way and to be starting to take an interest in her appearance. Your daughter is still young emotionally, but at eleven may be entering the first stages of womanhood physically. Puberty comes early these days. But, unless she is encouraged to use make-up skillfully, she is bound to apply it clumsily and present a clown-like appearance. Why not try a compromise? Perhaps let her wear it for parties and other special occasions, and let her have a demonstration by one of the consultants at a beauty counter as a treat so that she sees the natural look that a professional touch can achieve, and how much more attractive this is than several layers of paint and powder.

What you should most certainly *not* do is to tell her that under no circumstances must she paint her face. Denial without reason is always ineffective and will only encourage her to rebel. Be sure not to laugh at her first attempts either, however awkward they seem.

It is always something of a shock for a father to see his daughter growing into womanhood with all this implies. Maybe it is not so much that you dislike the make-up, but that you feel this is a reminder that within only a few years she may be ready to leave the nest.   J.G.

Q Do you think that our fourteen-year-old son is old enough to go off on a bicycle trip with a friend?

Candidly, few boys of that age have sufficient discretional ability to distinguish between what is safe and what is dangerous, and what is wise and what is foolhardy. However advanced a teenager is academically, this does not automatically imply that judgment and experience have reached an equal level of development. But a bicycle trip is certainly an exciting prospect. Why not join them, if you feel fit enough? That way, they will have the benefit of a responsible adult's supervision. In fact, it would provide an ideal opportunity for father and son to meet as individuals and to share a holiday adventure. When was the last time you spent some time together in this way? You will probably greatly enjoy the experience, too. Children do reach a stage when the straightforward family vacation becomes a boring prospect, which is why camp and other activity holidays are so often recommended.   J.G.

Q Do you think that it is ever better, in the instance of divorce, for a father to have custody of his child?

On the whole, the courts more often decide that a child will be better off with his or her mother. But a growing number of fathers are receiving custody. The aim of the court is always to provide the most stable and loving home environment for the child.

Whatever the situation, both parents need to do everything they can to avoid the child feeling that he or she is the object of a tug-of-war. And whatever the outcome, providing there are no contraindications, access to the noncustodial parent will be permitted on a regular basis. The courts realize the child's need for a father-figure. The father who really cares but who does not have custody will want to make the very most of his time with his child. Both parents need to make it clear that they have not divorced the child. J.G.

Q **How would you suggest that we handle our son's temper tantrums?**

A true temper tantrum is a fearful sight. It can happen at home or away, and sometimes there is no obvious cause. It is a situation of extreme frustration – the result of the child's inability to communicate his or her current emotion. The pent-up feelings become intolerable and the child literally goes ape.

It is a frightening experience for a parent and, quite understandably, for the child, too. It can also be extremely embarrassing if the tantrum occurs in a public place – a supermarket, for instance – and there is simply no controlling the child.

The important thing to remember is not to regress to the child's level emotionally by losing your temper, too, for there is a danger that his behavior may result in a seizure or breath-holding episode. A scolding or a quick swat will not work. He is himself already terrified by the emotion he is experiencing. So do not regress to his level emotionally, but do bend down to him physically. Forget your shopping or whatever else you were doing. Your child is the only thing that matters right now. Envelop him. Swaddle him. Take him within your physical orbit. Speak calmly, quietly, and slowly to him. Tell him you understand, that he shouldn't worry. In other words, apply an opposite in order to neutralize his emotions. With his tantrum, your child is crying out for help. His tantrum has complete control of him and he needs your reassuring physical presence to assuage it. For the very first time, perhaps, he has come to realize that someone else's wishes can conflict with his own.

Clearly, if you find a similar situation always arises in a particular environment, then you will have to avoid that environment. Some children, for instance, always seem to get trantrums in supermarkets. Perhaps the experience is too much for them, the crowds too frightening and noisy, the outing very boring and also tiring. Parenthood gives the greatest pleasures; it can also involve the hardest work at times, for father and mother. J.G.

Q **Is a child's sense of time very different from an adult's? To our six-year-old son, it would seem that a week is an eternity.**

Next week, next month, next year: there is very little distinction to a child for the first few years of life. It is also true, although there is little that can be offered by way of a scientific explanation, that time seems to pass more slowly in childhood. It may be that the days are not so full, it may be due to infantile impatience, and sometimes it is undoubtedly due to boredom. Many of us will recall having waited as school children for what appeared to be an inordinantly long period for a particularly tedious lesson to end.

You may have noticed, too, that your child – if told to wait for ten minutes – will come back repeatedly and ask if the time is up yet. To tell a small child, therefore, that you will do something *soon* is actually quite unfair because it has no real meaning for him. It will be far better if you can relate time to events whenever you can. To tell him you will do something *after* lunch, or *before* supper, or *as soon as* he gets up is far more sensible.

A week can certainly seem a very long time to a child. There are many incidents one could cite to illustrate this. Recently, I heard about one four-year-old who asked his mother where his father lived. His mother, completely mystified, replied that he lived with them, at home. Only later did she realize that her child did not see his father on a daily basis, because he would leave for work very early and return after the child's bedtime. The father saw his child on weekends, but to the child, last weekend was a very long while ago indeed.

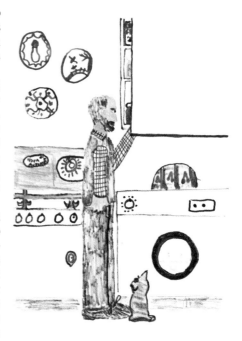

All this means that it is not a good idea to tell a child about some future event too far in advance. Don't let him get too excited weeks before his birthday or before Christmas. But if he does want to look forward to these occasions, you can help develop a sense of time by building a pile of bricks, perhaps, and removing one each day, or by doing the same sort of thing on a chalkboard, thus making time visual, much as an Advent calender does. Remember as well not to tell him too far in advance about a new brother or sister. Although he will need some preparation, telling him about the forthcoming event seven months in advance will be both unnecessary and unwise. He is bound to think the baby will never come and that it is all something of a story.   J.G.

In this tremendous area of concern, example is of paramount importance. Quite simply, if your children see you drinking, smoking a great deal, or taking drugs, they will not get the message.

You will also need to explain very carefully that use of soft drugs may in turn lead to further experimentation, often with very harmful consequences. It would be unwise to try to conceal in any way the horrors of such addiction. You might also choose to refer to the inadequacy of those individuals who turn to drugs in this way, and how the desperate need for drugs may lead to many forms of crime.

If your child ever appears drunk or hyperactive, or develops slurred speed, or seems to lose his or her inhibitions; if you notice money or objects suddenly disappearing from your house or apartment, or if there are sudden demands for money, you may have

Q One hears so many reports about glue-sniffing, drug-taking and alcoholism among young people. How would you suggest we best explain the dangers to our children?

reason to suspect that some form of drug-taking is at the root of the matter, in which case you have no alternative but to confront the problem .   M.G.

Q **How important do you think routine is to a child?**

Children, and most adults for that matter, come to rely upon routine for a sense of safety, and children feel particularly vulnerable when they do not know what to expect next. Take a class of seven-year-olds, for instance. If their regular teacher is sick for a couple of days, the children become very unsettled.

Change a child's routine at home and you are likely to meet with both emotional upset and resentment. Your children need routine as far as discipline and rules are concerned. They need to know where the perimeter fences are so that they can feel safe within them. Routine at bedtime is important as well, but I believe that bedtime should be a moveable feast. Indeed, to send children to bed when they are wide awake and full of energy seems to me to be a denial of their very individuality and needs. If you find yourself at times quite literally screaming at your child to go to bed, stop for a moment and think what effect this is having. Surely this will only be stimulating the child when what you actually should be trying to do is winding him or her down? Ideally, bedtime provides an opportunity for a father to spend a little time with his offspring, having a chat about the day's activities and perhaps reading a story together. Let this delightful end to the day become an important part of *your* routine, too.   J.G.

Q **How important do you regard the choice of name for a child?**

Some years ago, there was a very popular Country and Western song that told the amusing story of a boy named Sue who, not surprisingly, spent the whole of his adult life overcompensating for the handicap of his name. This is an extreme instance, and an amusing one, sure enough. But it does serve as an example of the importance with which all of us regard our name tags and the tremendous sense of personal identification set by them. That boy named Sue may have had a dreadful time trying to prove his strength and masculinity. So, in much the same way, a girl called Jackie (even if this is only short for Jacqueline) might end up either overcompensating simply to prove her femininity or perhaps taking up something of a more traditionally male stance in life.

This is, of course, a gross simplification. But it may help you see more clearly just how important names are. The fact that you are asking the question would indicate that you and your spouse are probably right now at variance about the choice of name for your child.

Names may not only suggest certain physical and personality characteristics – Faith, Prudence, Charity, Hope – they can also identify us with an era because of the element of fashion that comes into naming the baby. Since the birth of an heir to the British throne, for example, William has been repopularized as a name. But will your child be happy to be associated with a certain decade when he or she reaches middle age? Some names are also very suitable for the young, but hardly match a full-grown adult. Others may be ideal for someone of a definite physical build but ridiculous for anyone tall or short, slim or very large.

Certain names also undoubtedly lend a sense of dignity, and indeed if you were to draw up a list of successful people, you would probably find that many have strong-sounding names. Of course, a number of them would have risen to the top anyway because of innate ability but with another name, it could well have meant that, although head and shoulders above their competitors, they would have had to start from a hole in the ground.

If there is an unattractive family name that you feel bound to give your child for some reason – perhaps in memory of a grandparent or favorite aunt – consider giving it as a second name or choose a variation on the theme. Some people do manage to change their given names in adult life, but others sometimes feel that it is a rather pretentious thing to do, at least in the eyes of friends and colleagues. Some would even find it tantamount to rejection of their parents. Watch, too, that you do not give your child embarrassing initials or a name with some strange meaning in another language, and that the first name balances well with your surname. Give careful thought to the naming of your baby. It is most likely to be a present that you give him or her for life.   J.G.

It seems clear that your wife is having a problem handling your children's behavior and you are going to have to talk this through together very carefully because there are several aspects to this very obvious abdication of responsibility on her part – aspects that could, in the long-term, affect not only *her* relationship with the children quite deeply, but *yours* too.

She is, of course, indicating that she as an individual is simply not strong enough to handle the situation – not only physically but mentally and emotionally – so that a child may come to interpret this as a normal female behavior pattern, with the adult male always taking on the dominant role. Do you always want to be seen in this way? Should your children dread their father's arrival home when, instead of delighting at your coming through the door, they hide away upstairs or cower in the corner? How can you possibly consider the right sort of punishment when you are tired at the end of a long day and when the misdemeanor took place so many hours ago?

Here, in many ways, lies the crux of the problem. Your wife is actually, in delaying punishment, doling out a very harsh sentence on the children. From early infancy, we are indoctrinated to expect cause and

 My wife very often tells our children off when they are naughty by saying that I will punish them when I get home from work. Quite frankly, I find this very difficult.

effect as far as behavior is concerned. We are naughty, we know we should get punished, we usually are, the slate is wiped clean, we are no longer guilty. But any perod of anticipation, any delay in being punished, is usually more worrying than the punishment itself. In using your homecoming as a delaying tactic in this way, your wife is increasing the children's punishment possibly beyond all reason, maybe even outrageously.

Children come to rely on this aspect of cause and effect. In talking the matter over, try to emphasize this to your wife. Encourage her to issue a punishment of some kind there and then if she needs to do so. If it takes the form of denial of something, she must also see this through. A child needs total dependence on authority, and will only develop respect if the adult keeps his or her word, even if it is in a negative context.   J.G.

Q Our eight-year-old has received a very bad school report. Apparently he is lazy and his work is presented in a very untidy way. How can we best set about getting him to make a determined effort for the new school year?

You can tell him he is useless, he is ignorant, and he has shamed you: that way, you can be certain that next term's report will be pretty much the same. Alternatively, you can tell him it doesn't really matter and appear rather indifferent. Meanwhile, set about an improvement program using special tactics that he probably will not recognize as such and that will therefore be all the more effective in trying to get him to make more of an effort.

How often do you praise your child for something he has done well? How often do you even ask what he has done at school, what he is reading, or what he has had to do for homework? Whenever you find he has done something that shows an improvement, a reward of some kind, it is a good idea to remember, would not be out of place.

If his work has suddenly deteriorated, you obviously need to ask yourself what has caused the problem. If historically his work has been satisfactory, is there something disturbing him at school or at home, since these are the only two orbits in which he is functioning? Is he perhaps regressing as a response to the birth of a new baby? Is he using an attention-seeking mechanism? To do badly at school may be preferable to being ignored by you. Does he feel safe? Or is he worried by parental discord of some kind?

If, on the other hand, his work has been unsatisfactory for a long while now, there could be a learning problem. He may need to be assessed by an educational psychologist, or he may do better at another type of school. There could be other difficulties, too, of which you are unaware. Has he a hearing problem? Can he see the chalkboard? Is there a problem with his metabolism so that he lacks energy? It could be that there is some physical problem along these lines that has not yet been recognized.

Very often, however, it is not the child who does not

understand who receives a bad report but a child who is bored and needs more of a challenge in the classroom. This child, too, may require a different sort of school environment and method of teaching if he is to make good progress.

But the very fact that you are surprised by your child's end-of-term report is also worrying. Why have you only discovered this now? Was there no parent-teacher meeting earlier in the year? Was there no opportunity to discuss his progress with the teachers? Make a point of arranging to see your child's teacher or principal at the beginning of the new school year. Don't just turn up, but make an appointment. That way, the meeting is more likely to yield results as the staff will have had time to investigate your child's past work and discuss it with you thoroughly. A meeting that yields no more than a promise to look into the matter is a useless one. Try to find out how you can help at home to better his school work. In instances where parents show little interest, children are often disinclined to make an effort. Or maybe you have been pushing him too hard? Could it be that you demand too much of him? A bad school report is sometimes just as much an indictment on the parents as it is on the child.   J.G.

Keeping a promise to a child is not important: it is mandatory. The only other option is to become a liar, a cheat, or a thief to your child. Tell him or her you will do something and fail to do so, and you are lying. Go one further and get your child to act on the assumption that you will do that thing, and you are cheating him or her. What is more, in the child's eyes, you may have stolen the reward the child thought would justly be his or hers; that makes the child see you as a thief.

So always make it a golden rule *not* to make promises you feel you cannot keep and may therefore regret.

But promises are not always positive. Sometimes they can be used in a negative way and become a threat as a common parental weapon against bad behavior. The same rule should apply here, too. Again, only make promises you feel able to keep, and if that means withdrawing pocket money if your child does something you have explicitly asked him or her not to do, then withdrawn that pocket money definitely must be.

Children need to develop a sense of security as they grow. Knowing that there is someone in their immediate environment who is utterly honest and whose reactions are not irrational is a tremendous help in this respect. By always keeping your promises, you will be demonstrating a worthwhile mode of life by example. Keeping your promise reinforces the fact that you love your child, even if that promise is a negative one.   J.G.

 How important do you think it is for a parent always to keep his or her promise?

The *Weekend* *Father*

How often do you see your children? How much time
do you manage to spend with them? The scenario of
the father who find himself leaving for work before his
child gets up, and returning when he is already
asleep, is all too familiar today; it is not just the
separated or divorced parent who is with his child
only at weekends.

But a child needs a father figure, most psychologists
agree. Read on for some suggestions on weekend and
holiday activities. These should go a long way
towards bringing greater parental involvement when
there *is* a chance for father and child to be together.
Ideas for games to play both in the car and at birthday
parties as well as advice about safety in the home and
emergency firstaid also follow.

If you are aware, as are so many of today's fathers, that you are virtually married to your work and see precious little of your children, then taking the kids on a special short vacation each year, specifically so that you can get to know one another better, is certainly a great idea. But how much better not to leave furtherment of the father-child relationship to seven days out of three hundred and sixty-five. Putting aside a few hours each weekend specifically for your children will be far more beneficial for everyone. Make it a resolution. Don't let the pressures at work make you a stranger to your child. Spend a little time together each weekend. The chances are you, too, will reap many benefits into the bargain as you unwind. Have fun with your young family. These are golden years that can never be recaptured.

Family outings

Children of four and over definitely like having something to look forward to doing with their parents on weekends. It is as well, however, not to tell them about some planned activity too far in advance, if only because children have a completely different time scale from our own, so that a week can seem an absolute eternity away. You will be wise, too, always to have mentioned an alternative activity just in case it rains and the outing you had originally planned requires fine weather.

If you have a widely spaced family, there is quite an art in planning a successful outing, not only as far as your destination is concerned but also in ensuring that there is some aspect of the day you are spending together that is suitable for all age groups. The alternative will be for you to split up, for your wife or partner to take the younger children out and for you to go on an outing with the older ones, or vice versa. Remember, too, always to have an alternative outing or activity in mind, just in case your child suddenly doesn't like the idea of what you have planned. Kids sometimes get moody this way. If your child suddenly says he would rather stay at home, then this is probably what you ought to do, or you may find yourself with a grumpy youngster on tow all day. A child, on the other hand, cannot appreciate that adults, too, have moods. So unless you really feel unwell or there is some other immediate pressure, do everything you can to keep your promise as to an outing together. Your child may not have seen you throughout the week, yet will probably all the while have been thinking hard about the prospect of having you to himself or herself for two whole days.

Special children's films, puppet theaters and shows, young people's theater workshops, children's concerts, leisure and arts centers – all offer a wealth of family entertainment. Check your local newspaper for details of such weekend activities in your vicinity. River and lake trips, too, are fun for the over-fours. As always, but on the water particularly, you will need to keep safety to the forefront of your mind.

Even those children living in towns will enjoy a sightseeing tour, as long as you do not make this too lengthy since a child's attention span is not that elastic. And, of course, a trip to the nearest big city for the child who is being brought up in a country environment will always be thrilling.

All children love the zoo, and will probably enjoy a visit at least once a year, if you are able to plan one. Try to go at feeding time; children find this particularly fascinating. There may also be a special children's section, featuring rides and an opportunity to meet certain tame animals at close quarters.

An outing to a museum will also be enjoyable, and even a child as young as four years of age will find lots to interest him or her in many collections. Some museums even organize special children's sessions and competitions, and will have working models for young people to operate. Before you plan your outing, call and find out whether there are any particular children's activities at special times. Bear in mind not only the major national museums, but smaller specialist collections, too – railway and toy museums, for instance. A visit to your nearest international airport, to view take-off and landings from a special platform, can also be exciting to a small child. Even when time is short, a visit to a local park or playground can still serve as something of a treat if you turn the occasion into an adventure by bringing along a picnic. Take along a small boat to sail, if the park has a lake, or a kite to fly, if the wind is favorable. (The exercise will do you good, too!) At recreation and sports centers you will also be able to enjoy swimming and ice skating together. The trend is now for infants to learn to swim as young as possible, and children as young as four years of age have been known to take quite readily to the ice.

It may not always be possible to bring along a packed lunch. If this is the case, you will need to find a restaurant that caters to children. If you find one of the several big hamburger or pizza chains, well and good (if, that is, you enjoy this sort of food yourself!). Alternatively, you should find that many other establishments also have junior menus, and even special seating for the very young, as well as facilities for warming a baby's bottle. If your child is not used to eating out, it will be sensible not choose anywhere too grand.

Remember that small children usually find walking a long way very tiring: so it will definitely be wise from everyone's point-of-view to have the stroller or buggy with you, and to make use of it as soon as necessary. You may also find that your young child wants to bring along with him a special toy or doll, or a favorite piece of cloth or blanket. This may seem unnecessary to you, but for your child it will possibly provide a great source of comfort. The most successful family outings undoubtedly require a certain amount of advance planning where young children are concerned.

Shopping with children

Like many fathers, you may find yourself assisting with the grocery shopping on Saturday. A number of people find this a dreadful chore, particularly if they have to bring small children along. But there are several things you can do to make the expedition an eventless and even quite enjoyable one.

Firstly, it will help if you can be carrying a small infant, rather than having him or her in a stroller. A sling is particularly useful for shopping, and there are several sorts on the market that will enable you to remain in close and reassuring contact with the baby, even while he or she is asleep. A rucksack with a rigid frame and worn on the back is also handy for an older child who will enjoy looking out at his or her surroundings. Once your child is walking, you may like to have him or her on reins when shopping, so that he or she cannot wander off. Or use the seat in the grocery cart. The trick is to shop as early as you can, when the store is less likely to be crowded. If your child is forever handling products on the shelves, you will need to exert a little discipline, and it is wise to keep the cart in the center of the aisle. Never leave a child in a buggy or stroller outside the store, or alone near the checkout, and tell your child not to leave the supermarket if by chance you get separated. If you both dress in something brightly colored, it will be easier to spot one another.

Shopping can also provide some useful lessons for an older child. Take advantage of the occasion to show him or her how to compare prices and value, weight for weight and size for size. Explain why you opt for a small, economy, or jumbo size as far as certain items are concerned. Let him or her cross off the items on your shopping list. Encourage your child, too, to help with unloading the cart and checking any change you are given.

If your children are given spending money on a regular basis, it could well be that, while you are out, they will want to spend some of it. You should already have come to a definite understanding as to who pays for what. This being the case, to whatever extent you feel your child is wasting his or her pocket money on something, you can do nothing other than offer advice if you have actually said that the child can buy what he or she likes with the money.

One way around the problem, some parents find, is to insist that children save half of what you give them. In fact, a regular weekly visit to a bank, so that a child can put something into his or savings account, is a worthwhile thing for the family to do together.

By going shopping together, you can also help educate your child as a consumer from from a very early age. When buying something for a new baby, for instance, explain to an older child why you are checking to see that there are no sharp edges and that it is nontoxic. Point out why certain toys are more interesting and why others are likely to be five-minute wonders (though you'll doubtless, like all parents,

end up buying a few of these, too.) And do explain if certain items are beyond your budget. There is no harm at all in this. In fact, coming to understand that not everything is always available to us is a very important lesson, best learnt early on.

Take special care when crossing the street while shopping, as you should on all occasions when out with a child. Set an example by doing so only at the traffic lights or crosswalks. Let your child explain to you the safety precautions he or she is taught at school, but be prepared that, from eight years upwards, your child may be a little too independent to hold your hand. Nevertheless, he or she should cross right by you, and assist you in helping any younger brother or sister to cross, so that you all do so together.

Out in the car

Traveling by car is undoubtedly the easiest way of getting about with kids. But there are certain all-important safety factors you must at all costs bear in mind as far as each child passenger is concerned. First and foremost, *never* allow an adult to travel in the front seat with either a baby or a toddler on his or her knee. An infant can be left in an infant seat, but this should be fastened with special safety straps to the back seat. There are several designs of car seats for the child who can sit up. Again, always ensure this is securely fastened and at the back of the car, and that a safety belt is incorporated. Take great care, too, when shutting the car doors. Children have a curious knack of getting their fingers in the way.

You will need to set certain behavior rules for older children when traveling by car, because squabbling, noisy play and restlessness can be annoying to the driver, and even dangerous. Stop to give everyone a chance to stretch their legs at least once every hour. Don't encourage eating in the car: far better that you stop for a snack every now and then. This should help prevent unnecessary car sickness, as will an open window, unless it is very cold, or airconditioning. Check, too, that childproof locks are in operation. On a long journey, simple games can help enormously to keep a child happily occupied. Here are just a few that children find entertaining.

Fizz, buzz

Each player has a turn in counting upwards, but whenever five, a multiple of five, or a number featuring a five is reached, the player whose turn it is must say "fizz" instead of that number. You can make the game more complicated by additionally substituting "buzz" for "seven" in the same way.

Spot them all!

Make up a list of about ten items that are likely to be seen on your trip. These might include police officers, a bridge, a hospital, a horse, an Alsatian dog, someone using a cane, someone pushing a stroller, an ice-cream vendor, a fire engine, and a street musician. Give each child a copy of the list. The goal is to cross off as many of the items as possible by the end of the trip. Score one point for every item spotted.

What's my line?

One player has to think up a job, trade, or profession, and the others have to guess what this is by asking questions, to which only the answers "yes" or "no" may be given. "Do you work indoors?" "Do you make something?" "Could I ask you to do this for me?" These are examples of questions that may be asked, and just ten are allowed. This is, of course, an adaptation of the well-known television game.

Highway code

Provide one copy of the Highway Code for each child, or alternatively simply some photostats of the pages illustrating the principal road signs. The goal is to find as many different signs as possible along the route, and to cross them off as they are spotted.

Lucky numbers

Before the journey, each child chooses a number with up to four digits. The idea is to see how many vehicles he or she can find with exactly the same number combination on the license plate.

Snap!

This is a variation on the well-known children's card game. Each player in turn names a make and color of car – a green Mercedes or a white Cortina, for instance. When another player spots a car of this description, he or she must shout "Snap!" and it will then be his or her turn to name a car.

Count the lights

Counting the number of traffic lights you pass through without having to stop because they are green will also keep your young passengers happily occupied. Don't let their enthusiasm force you into speeding or taking risks in order to catch the lights, however!

Alphabet games

There are many games that can be played on this theme, and they will be suitable for children of five years and over. Choose a subject – countries, towns, girls' or boys' names, or animals, for instance. The first player starts with, say, a town beginning with A (Amsterdam maybe), and the next player must think of a town beginning with its last letter (Manchester perhaps). Any player unable to continue after two minutes' thinking time is "out".

I-spy

This is a guessing game that requires both knowledge of the alphabet and good observational powers. One child will say "I-spy, with my little eye, something beginning with T" or whatever letter is appropriate, and the others must try to guess the object in question. The player who guesses correctly takes the next turn.

Name that tune!

This is a wonderful game for keeping two or three children quiet. They simply have to mouth the words of a well-known song silently, and the test is whether the other player or players can lipread the words correctly and name that tune.

Car license numbers

As soon as they can read, your children should enjoy spotting license numbers and making suggestions as to what phrases the initials might stand for. Other car number games include spotting a number beginning with A, B, and so on, or a numerical progression.

Counting games

Pick a subject – police officers, ambulances, dogs, or people wearing hats, for instance – and the children count how many they each spot on the trip.

Happy birthday!

Most children like to show off their fathers. The chances are that their friends already know their mothers quite well, meeting on the way to or from school, when shopping, or when invited to play during the week. But father remains a figure only spoken about – until, that is, an opportunity like a birthday party presents itself, so that everyone can become acquainted.

Birthday parties are tremendous fun to plan, and almost all fathers enjoy lending a hand, if not taking over completely, so these occasions are best held on weekends or during a vacation, no matter if the date does not coincide exactly with the birthday. Parties for one- and two-year-olds are really no more than adult get-togethers. But come the third birthday, children are far more social.

If your child has come home from other kids' parties, full of stories about an elaborate affair with a magician, puppet theater presentation, a lavish dinner, or even a disco, don't be convinced that you must provide professional entertainment too, when it comes to your own celebration. It is perfectly possible to organize a really successful party on a shoestring budget. In fact, many of the parties that children enjoy the most are often the most simple.

The excitement starts with sending out the invitations. To cut costs, and to produce something more original and attractive for the young recipients, make your own designs for cards. If your child is four years of age or over, you could work on these together. Get some brightly-colored cardboard, and draw a strong basic shape (a house, a teddy bear, a gingerbread man, a rabbit, or a clown, for instance). This can then be cut out, and the invitation details written in felt-tip pen. More elaborate cards can also be made. You might try a design that folds and stands up on its own, one that folds in a zig-zag shape, or even one that has to be assembled like a puzzle before the invitation can be read. You need to send out invitations about three weeks in advance. If you cannot invite everyone in your child's class at school, as is often the case, it may be best to mail the invitations to home addresses, or to give them out discreetly after school. (Make sure you have everyone's home address or telephone number anyway, in case you have to cancel the party at the last moment because of illness or an emergency.) Make it clear, too, on the invitation what sort of party it is to be. If you are holding it outdoors, for example, the activities may not be so much fun for children who turn up in their best clothes. And remember to give the time you would like your guests to be picked up. Fasten some balloons to the front door. This makes a grand welcome, and is a sure sign that the guests have come to the right address.

It is an excellent idea to plan a theme for the party and, if you do, this can be indicated on the invitation. Themes that have proved successful with the under-eights include a space party (with invitations in the shape of rockets, and the party room and table decorated with stars and planets), a masked party (provide each young guest with an animal mask on arrival), and a fancy dress party (usually most popular with girls). In only an hour and with just a little imagination, colored paper, crepe paper, silver foil, and balloons, you should be able to transform the party room into any one of a whole range of fantasy environments.

Make sure that you clear the room in which the party is to be held of all objects that might be dangerous or that could get broken. Check, too, that you have a first aid kit handy, in case of mishaps, and avoid having an open or gas fire. It's wise, too, to take any key out of the bathroom door, for fear of a guest getting locked in, and to lock those doors of any rooms in which you definitely do not want the children to play.

There is no getting around the problem: a party for the under-eight age group is likely to be a messy affair. A paper or plastic cloth, lots of paper napkins, and disposable plates and cups are therefore the order of the day. If the weather is likely to be fine, and you are fortunate enough to have a yard, hold the party outdoors, and serve food picnic-style. Small children are perfectly happy sitting cross-legged on a large rug. The real secret of an unforgettable birthday party is, of course, the cake, and although it will probably be more delicious if made at home, you will also be able to transform even the most ordinary of basic chocolate or simple white cakes into a castle or fort, a galleon, an ark, or a rocket with imaginative use of colored icing, candies, cookies, and chocolates, with colored paper, ribbon, small toys, and candles used as decorations.

Like most fathers, you will probably find organizing and helping out at your child's birthday party exhausting but tremendous fun.

Keep the food itself as simple as possible. Small children often feel sick after parties, a combination of too much excitement and too many sweet things to eat being the most likely cause. Hot dogs, hamburgers, pizza and ice cream sundaes remain firm favorites, and you will need plenty of juices. Children tend to get thirsty at parties, so you will do well to have plenty in reserve.

Remember, too, that not all parties have to be held in the afternoon. Older children might enjoy a dinner party, or perhaps a brunch, or even a barbecue, although the latter will require careful supervision.

Birthday celebrations can also take other forms, and you may sometimes opt not to make the occasion at home but to organize an outing – to a children's show, the zoo, or a museum, for instance. This can be just as much fun, but do remember that coping with a crocodile of energetic six- or seven-year-olds can be quite demanding, particularly if you have to travel with them to your destination on public transport. They are bound to get hungry on such a trip, so not only will you need to bring along snacks, but you will probably also want to take them to a restaurant for something suitably festive to eat. Outings of this kind are fairly ambitious undertakings if the group extends to more than six; if it does, you will probably need the help of one other adult.

Games to play

Now to the area where fathers really come into their own: the organization of party games. It is usually best to have these at the beginning of the party, before the meal, both to get everyone into a lively mood and to avoid tummy upsets, reserving quieter entertainment, like a story, for later. In case it is some years since you last played host to a gang of small children, the following list of basic party games may be helpful. Most are suitable for three-year-olds and over. Small prizes for each winner will be well received.

What's in the box?

Prepare a large square box in advance, and make four openings in the sides. Each opening should be large enough for a child's hand. Then make four divisions inside the box, and seal the top. Place four different objects in each opening: a flower, a feather, a cookie and a key, for instance. Each player has to reach inside the box and whisper to you what each object is, simply by touching it. Have a small prize for four correct guesses.

Squeak, piggy, squeak

All the children sit in a circle on the floor. One player is chosen to be blindfolded. He is spun round and then has to find his way from the center of the circle to a seated player. He sits on his lap, and says "Squeak, piggy, squeak". The aim is to guess the name of the player by the sound of his or her voice.

What was on the tray?

This is a memory game, and suitable only for an older age group since answers must be written. Place a selection of objects on a tray – things like a key, a spoon, a ring, an apple, a coin, a cup, and a pen. Twelve objects in all is a good number. Let the guests look at the tray for about two minutes, as they try to memorize the objects. Then take the tray away, and get them to write down all the objects they can remember. The winner is the player who remembers most objects correctly. (You may need more than one prize for this game.)

Pass the package

Prepare the package before the party by wrapping a small present in several layers of paper. Recycle used gift paper and newspaper for this. All your young guests should sit in a circle, preferably on the floor. Play some lively music, and get them to pass the package around the circle. When the music stops, the child who is holding the package should unwrap just one layer of paper. Start the music again, and repeat.

The child who takes off the final layer receives the present. It may be as well to prepare several parcels, as the children may want to play this popular game three or four times.

Musical statues

Play some music and get the children to jump up and down. When you stop the music, everyone should stand as still as possible. Anyone who moves is "out", until you are left with just one contestant who is the winner.

Musical bumps

This is a variation on *musical statues*. Once again, play some music. When it suddenly comes to a halt, all the children must immediately sit on the floor. Anyone who sits down before the music stops is "out", and so is the last player to sit down. Again, the last player left is the winner.

Musical chairs

Set out a row of chairs, facing alternate ways, with one less chair than the number of players. Play some lively music, and get the children to dance around the row of chairs. The player who doesn't manage to sit down is "out". With each round of the game, remove one chair. The final remaining player is the winner.

Pin the tail on the donkey

If you have a chalkboard or easel (see page 54), draw a large picture of a donkey, without a tail. Alternatively, fasten a drawing of a donkey to a door or wall. Now cut out a tail for the donkey. Blindfold each child in turn, and get him or her to try to fasten the tail in the correct position on the donkey.

Pass the orange

Divide your guests into two teams. Give each team an orange. The goal is for the orange to be placed under the first child's chin, and for it to be passed along the line, without anyone using his or her hands. It should cause much merriment!

Obstacle race

You will need to let each child run the course individually and time him or her, or set a similar course for each child so that they can run the race simultaneously. This sort of race is really only suitable for outdoors, and you will need several obstacles to place at various stops – a small object to be jumped over, a rope to climb under, clothes to put on and take off, and some stepping stones, for instance. Take care not to include anything dangerous.

Egg and spoon race

This game, too, is suitable only for playing outdoors. Mark out starting and finishing lines, and give each player a large spoon and a hardboiled egg, or use potatoes. Each player has to balance an egg or potato on the spoon, hold it in one hand only, and run to the finishing line. If a child drops the egg or potato, he or she can pick it up but must use only one hand to do so.

Smell it! Taste it!
You will need to blindfold each player, and present him or her with various foodstuffs to smell and identify. Examples of the items you could use are a lemon, chocolate, fish, and scented soap. In a second round, you can get them to identify tidbits of food by taste, while still blindfolded: honey, potato, apple, and radish, for instance. Score one point for each correct answer.

How many are there?
In advance, prepare a large jar of nuts, cheese straws, or candies, counting them as you fill the jar. Ask your young guests to guess how many it contains. Present the jar to whoever gives the nearest number (and perhaps suggest that the contents are handed round).

Red, Green, Yellow, Blue
Pin four large differently colored pieces of paper or balloons in each of the four corners of the room. Play some music. When it stops, the children have to run to whichever corner they choose. You hide your eyes and call out one color. All the children in that particular corner are then "out". Continue until either one or no players are left "in".

O'Grady says
Standing in front of the children, give them all instructions, stating "O'Grady says: jump up and down!" or "O'Grady says: raise your right arm!" for instance. The young players should do exactly what you say, but must *not* do so if you fail to state "O'Grady says" before the command. You will have to declare that anyone who does so is "out".

Capitals
Divide your guests into two teams, and provide each with twelve identical small pieces of paper, on six of which are the names of countries, and on the other six the corresponding capitals. Give them three minutes to match up each of the six pairs, side by side.

Yes sir! No sir!
Divide the players into two teams. Then taking each team in turn, ask each player a question, which he or she must answer without using the words "yes" or "no". Whoever does so is "out".

Matching pairs
Cut out from magazines and newspapers photographs of famous couples. Divide your young guests into two teams, and give them each a set of ten pictures to pair into sets of five. Examples might include Ronald and Nancy Reagan, Prince Charles and Princess Diana, Popeye and Olive Oil, Tom and

Jerry, Laurel and Hardy, Donald Duck and Mickey Mouse, Kermit and Miss Piggy. If each team is given different sets of pictures, they can then play another round with the other set. Three minutes should be adequate for each round.

You can adapt this game by giving each child a name label at the beginning of the party, and getting him or her to find the appropriate partner. This is a particularly good way of encouraging shy children to get to know one another.

Charades
The children should first be divided into two teams. Each team is then given the title of a book or film and asked to mime the title to the other team who will try to guess it. Set a time limit of three minutes for a secret rehearsal of each mime and a further three minutes for the performance. Award one point for each correct guess.

Three-legged race
This game is best played out-of-doors. Divide the children into pairs. Stand them next to one another, and tie one child's inside leg to the other's inside leg, using a large handkerchief or piece of cloth. Mark out starting and finishing lines, and see which three-legged pair wins.

Pass the balloon
Divide the guests into two teams, and give the child at the head of each line a long balloon. The first child then has to put the balloon between his or her knees and pass it to the next child without either of them touching it with his or her hands. You may need some spare balloons.

Comics
Provide one comic or newspaper for each child, having previously put the pages out of sequence. The first player to put the pages together in the correct order will be the winner. To be fair, check that each comic has the same number of pages.

Who are they?
Collect a number of pictures of well-known people and pin them to a board. Each child then has to guess who they are. Try to include sportsmen, actors, pop stars and other men and women they are likely to recognize.

Lucky dip
Wrap a small present for each guest and place them in a large box. You can then invite each child to have a 'lucky dip' for a gift to take home as a memento.

Sack race
Provide a sack for each child and mark starting and finishing lines. Each child has to get into the sack and jump his or her way along the course.

Safety First

Research repeatedly reveals that most childhood accidents occur within the home. Rather than being wise after the event, you really ought to make sure your house or apartment is as childproof as it should be. The weekend is an ideal time to take care of this, and the following is an outline list of the all-important points to bear in mind, particularly as far as very young children are concerned.

In the kitchen
- is the floor nonslip?
- do you store all potentially dangerous substances safely out of reach?
- are the saucepan handles always turned inwards?
- are you careful never to put any poisonous substance in a differently labeled container?
- do you ensure your child is out of the way when the ironing is being done?
- are there any dangerous cords?
- do you avoid using tablecloths that a child might grab?
- are all sharp implements and matches safely out of reach?
- are there any plastic bags around that could cause suffocation?

In the bathroom
- are there razor blades lying around?
- are you careful never to leave a small child alone in the bathtub?
- do you always check the temperature of the water before bathing your child?
- is the medicine cabinet childproof?
- is the floor nonslip?
- do you ask the pharmacist for childproof medicine bottles?

The bedroom
- is your child's nightwear inflammable?
- are you careful not to give a pillow to a baby of under one year of age?
- are there safety catches or bars on the windows?
- can the cupboard doors be opened from inside?
- are there any medicines or cosmetics lying around that your child might get hold of?
- do you always remember to remove a hot water bottle before your small child goes to bed?

The hall and stairs
- are the hall and stairs well lit?
- are there switches at top and bottom?
- do you need a safety gate, for use once your baby starts to crawl?
- are the banisters secure?
- if the banisters have bars, are they wide enough apart so that they are not a potential danger?
- is there a loose mat that might cause a fall at the bottom of the stairs?

Check those stairs. Are they a potential danger to your child now that he or she is walking? A safety gate may be a wise precaution. Check that the banisters are secure, too.

The living room
- if you have a fireplace, is it properly guarded?
- do you have dummy plugs that fit into the electric sockets so that they are not a danger to your child once he or she is crawling and they become an object of curiosity?
- are you careful to place precious or breakable objects out of reach?
- do you always remember to place hot liquids like tea or coffee well away so that they cannot be spilled on a baby or toddler?
- do you lock away any alcohol?
- are you careful not to leave cigarettes lying around as they can be dangerous to a toddler?

Outdoors
- is the yard enclosed and the gate always shut, preferably with a childproof latch?
- are there any shrubs, trees, or plants in the garden that are poisonous?

- is any garden pond or swimming pool a potential danger to your child?
- is the garage kept locked?
- is the car kept locked?
- is there any old kitchen equipment lying around that could be a dangerous hiding place?

The first aid kit

While prevention is, of course, always better than cure, it is impossible to avoid the occasional cuts and bruises. It will therefore be wise to have to hand a good first aid kit and/or medicine cabinet. They should contain at least the following basics:

- cotton-tipped swabs, sterile gauze squares and bandages
- scissors, safety pins and square-ended tweezers
- thermometer
- children's aspirin subsitute
- antihistamine cream (for stings)
- antiseptic (for cleaning a wound)
- sun cream
- calamine lotion
- milk of magnesia (for stomach upsets)

Be sure that the medicine cabinet has a childproof lock, and that it is out of reach of toddlers. Any drugs and tablets no longer required should be flushed away. It is a good idea, too, to ensure that all medicines that are prescribed are in childproof bottles.

Here are some all-important points to bear in mind, and the action to take in case of certain accidents.

Bites

Be sure to see the doctor if ever your child is bitten by a dog or some other animal. Rabies will be the chief concern, and the doctor will want to know the date of the last tetanus injection. In case of a snake bite, lie the child down, see he does not move and call the doctor as a matter of urgency.

Blisters

Do not prick them. No treatment is necessary. The function of a blister is to protect the new skin. If the blister is liable to be rubbed, however, protect it with a dressing.

Bruises

The old remedies of rubbing butter on a bruise or putting a piece of steak on a black eye are not very helpful, but a cold compress or ice-pack applied to a bruise may relieve any swelling. Any severe bruising, however, should be shown to a doctor. It is advisable to show a black eye to a doctor, too.

Burns

It is important as far as babies and children are concerned that all but the most tiny burns are seen by

The kitchen is a particular danger spot as far as young children are concerned. Is all equipment kept safely out of reach? Are there any dangerous substances around?

the doctor, and that a child with a large burn should be taken to hospital at once. Simply hold a minor burn under cold, running water. This will ease the pain. Then cover it with clean gauze. Do not apply butter, soap or creams: these will not help at all. If clothing catches fire, wrap your child in a blanket or rug and pour on cold water. Do not remove any burned clothing unless the burn is due to scalding with a liquid. In this case, remove your child's clothes and wrap him in a clean sheet before taking him to hospital. *See also Sunburn.*

Chilling

Newborn babies lose body heat very quickly. They therefore need to be in a warm environment. A baby may be chilled, remember, even if his hands and face look normal. If he is chilled, his stomach will feel cold. A severely chilled baby needs prompt medical help. If you cannot get to a doctor or hospital quickly, try warming the baby through body contact in a warm room.

Choking

Peanuts and candy are often the culprits. Hold your child upside down and slap his back fairly smartly between the shoulder blades. Alternatively, for a baby, you can lie him on his back, put both hands round him and give three or four pushes with your thumbs. You can also try this for an older child, sitting him in a chair. If this is not successful, try putting your fingers down his throat or seek medical help at once. *(See pages 24-25)*

Convulsions

Convulsions can sometimes be a sign of epilepsy, and certain other conditions. But they may also occur as a result of a sudden raise in a child's temperature. Any fit which occurs should be reported to a doctor at once: and if it continues for more than two minutes, it should be regarded as an emergency. Place your child so that his head is to one side so that, if he vomits, he will not choke. Stay with him, and if he has a raised temperature, sponge him down to cool him.

Cramp

Get your child to stretch the muscle as hard as possible. The best treatment for cramp in the calf is to stand on the leg and to press down on the foot. Massage may also help.

Cuts

Cleanse all cuts and grazes thoroughly, using an antiseptic. Dress the wound. See the doctor or go to the emergency room of the nearest hospital if the wound is very deep. To stop severe bleeding, place pressure above the wound, and raise an injured limb above heart level.

Electric shock

A mild electric shock is experienced as a tingle. But a severe shock can cause unconsciousness and may even stop breathing. First of all, switch off the current or pull out the plug. Be sure not to touch the casualty because you will get a shock yourself. In some circumstances, it may not be possible to reach the mains or the plug. In this case, push your child or the object away with anything that does not conduct electricity – that is, something wooden or rubber. If the child is unconscious, check his breathing. If this is fairly normal, place him in the recovery position *(see Unconsciousness)*. Otherwise, external cardiac massage or artificial respiration may be necessary. Call the doctor or telephone for an ambulance.

Finger injuries

Children quite often trap their fingers in a door, and this can be very painful. Putting the finger under a running, cold water tap for two minutes or so will help to relieve the pain a little and should reduce any bleeding. If the finger seems damaged, take your child to the hospital.

Fractures

If you suspect a fracture, do not move your child more than necessary. Having dealt with any external bleeding, if medical help is delayed, make a temporary splint by wrapping a walking stick or umbrella alongside and well above and below the suspected break. Fasten it securely enough not to allow movement of the limb but not so tightly that blood flow is restricted.

Nosebleeds

Holding your child's head down, place pressure on either side of the nose until the bleeding stops. Then see he or she sits up, rather than lying down. An ice-pack on the bridge of the nose may also stop the bleeding. Tell your child to avoid blowing his nose for several hours after the bleeding has stopped.

Objects in the ears, eyes and nose

Any object in the ear should be removed by a doctor to avoid damage to the eardrum. Dust in the eyes will usually come out on its own when the eyes water. If anything else gets into the eye, seek prompt medical help. If it is a chemical, pour water over the eye and take the child to hospital at once. Try to stop your child from rubbing the eye. Do not apply a dressing. If your child gets an object stuck in his nose, try to get him to breathe through his mouth and seek medical help at once. Do not try to remove the object yourself.

Poisoning

Seek immediate medical help, and take along a sample of the substance you suspect your child has swallowed. If he or she has swallowed a household poison or a corrosive substance such as bleach, paint stripper or a cleaning fluid, you can safely give water in an attempt to dilute it, if he is conscious, but do not try to make the child sick. The vomit could damage the throat and lungs. Only try to make your child sick on your way to prompt medical help if he has swallowed something like a large quantity of pills or berries and is conscious. Do this by putting your fingers in his mouth and to the back of his throat. But do not keep trying if this does not work, and do not give an emetic like salt water in the attempt to make him vomit.

Shock

Your child may suffer from shock after a fright or injury and appear shaky with a pale face and clammy skin. Get him to lie down so that his head is lower than his feet. This will ensure that the blood is passing to the brain. Cover him with a blanket. Place his head to one side so that if he vomits, he will not choke. Do not offer anything to eat or drink until he feels better. Acute shock with symptoms of giddiness and rapid breathing should be treated by a doctor.

Splinters

You can remove a thorn or splinter by using a sterilized needle to break the skin at the end of the splinter. Then use tweezers to pull it out. If the splinter is very large and painful, see the doctor.

Sprains

If your child has discomfort on moving a joint and it appears swollen or bruised, it may be sprained. If the joint is too painful to move or to bear weight, see the doctor as soon as possible. In less extreme circumstances, to minimize both the swelling and the pain, raise the sprained joint and apply an ice-pack. A bandage to support the joint should also help, and the affected limb should be rested as much as possible. You might try putting your child's arm in a sling for a sprained elbow. This will certainly stop him using the arm for a while and thus rest the joint. If after forty-eight hours the joint is still troublesome, see the doctor.

Stings

In case of a bee sting, first clean the area around the sting with a cotton swab soaked in bicarbonate of soda, and then remove the sting with tweezers or a sterilized needle. Do not try to squeeze out the sting, or the poison may spread. See the doctor about a wasp or bee sting in the mouth, and report any allergic reaction such as swelling, dizziness or vomiting. Meanwhile, let your child either sip a very cold drink or suck an ice cube. An antihistamine cream will ease any irritation following either wasp or bee stings. For nettle stings, a dock leaf may have a cooling effect. Alternatively, use calamine lotion, an antihistamine cream or an ice-pack.

Sunburn

You should make sure that children are well protected from the risk of sunburn. Use a suntan cream with a high protective factor, and restrict exposure. Sunhats and umbrellas or sunshades will provide additional protection. In the event of mild sunburn, apply calamine lotion to soothe the discomfort. In case of bad sunburn, and particularly if your child has a raised temperature, feels ill or is blistered, consult a doctor.

Unconsciousness

Seek immediate medical help. Meanwhile, place your child in the recovery position: that is, on his side, with his upper arm at right angles to his body, bending his elbow. Draw up the thigh to form a right angle and bend his knee. Check that his mouth and nose are not blocked, that the tongue has not fallen to the back of the mouth, and that clothing is loose. If he is not breathing, use artificial respiration (mouth-to-mouth) or external cardiac massage, placing the heel of your hand on his breastbone and pressing for about a second, repeating in a regular rhythm.

The Absentee Father

Statistics show that some sixty percent of all divorces in the Unites States involve children, that thirty percent or so of all American children are not living at home with both parents, and that Europe doesn't lag far behind. The absentee father is thus by no means unusual, particularly as mothers are most often granted custody of any children.

Psychologists agree, however, that it is very important – for both father and child – for paternal contact to be maintained. There is evidence that children who maintain such a regular link are less likely to have emotional problems and more likely to relate more readily with others. There is, of course, no guarantee that, should you find yourself in such circumstances, your relationship with your children will be fine if you see them regularly, but it will certainly go a long way toward promoting more stability.

If, like many separated or divorced fathers, you are granted access only periodically, or on weekends, you will do well to bear in mind certain guidelines when you see your young family, both for their sake and your own.

- try to make each meeting a positive experience
- don't shower your children with presents, so that they come to think of you only in terms of gifts – affection cannot be bought
- try to keep exactly to any arrangements you make (children greatly resent any alteration in plans)
- try not to be late because a child may easily misconstrue this and feel that he or she is unimportant to you, or that you are unreliable
- if, for some reason, you are not able to get back on time, call and explain this to their mother as children may fear an angry reaction when they get home
- never bribe your child to see you; forced meetings are unlikely to be happy ones
- if your child is reluctant to see you, consider whether there is something else he or she would rather be doing, whether it is the influence of the other parent, or whether it is something the child doesn't like about your times together
- if you have remarried or are cohabiting, consider whether it may be best to spend some time alone with your child, or whether he or she is sufficiently confident about the situation to enjoy being with your new family
- take the trouble to find out what really interests your child
- keep a list of ideas for activities and outings
- make sure that you allow a certain amount of time to listen to what your child wants to tell you about what he or she has been doing
- do everything you can not to cancel arrangements unless absolutely essential: this can be very upsetting to a child

The Father Craftsman

Making simple items of furniture for the bedroom and playroom, as well as a variety of toys to encourage imaginative play, is not beyond the creative skills of even the most inexperienced woodworker. The exciting projects on the pages that follow are presented with both straightforward instructions and clear working diagrams, and all can be completed within just a couple of weekends, some much more quickly. All require only the most basic tools and the materials should be both easy to find and inexpensive to purchase. Welcome the newborn with a beautiful rocking cradle. Build him or her a practical highchair. Make a simple pull-along toy for a toddler, a dollhouse for a daughter, or a wheelbarrow for garden activities. Build a bird feeder for the enthusiastic young ornithologist or an easel for the junior artist. Let your child help you with construction of these and several other projects designed to please the young generation. Working together in this way should provide many happy hours of father-child companionship with end results that are bound to delight.

Tools and equipment

Most householders will be reasonably conversant with day-to-day home repairs, and almost certainly will have a basic set of tools, even if this extends only to a hammer, screwdriver, and an electric drill. However, now that so many of the things we buy are ready-made units, coupled with the fact that woodworking is no longer so widely taught in schools, most of us have only a basic knowledge of the techniques of construction. This has been taken into account in the projects presented on the pages that follow, so that even those entirely new to working in wood should find the instructions quite straightforward to understand. The following basic introduction to the use of woodworking tools should also prove useful.

It is often said that a bad workman always blames his tools. This may be true enough, but without good equipment, even the most proficient handyman will find it difficult to produce anything like a professional finish.

Good tools are, however, often expensive, so it is well worth spending a little time in selecting the right equipment from the outset. Don't make the false economy of buying the cheapest items you can find. Rather, choose the best that you can afford at the time of purchase. Well-made tools will give long and good service, and should last a lifetime.

If your knowledge is really elementary, the experts suggest that, before buying any tools, you should compare not only prices but also the extent to which you are comfortable holding different tools. Weight and balance are important, and the right feel is a personal matter. If in doubt, it is always safer to choose a product made by an established manufacturer, but don't dismiss something simply because it is less expensive. If it seems to suit you and is finished well, it may just be a real bargain. Knowledge of what is right for the job is something that will increase will experience.

The workbench

Just as the actual tools that you use are important, so is the surface on which you are going to work. A great deal can be done on a table, but apart from the fact that the table will almost inevitably get damaged in time, some form of vise will be necessary to hold your work in position.

The ideal set-up is the traditional joiner's bench that is made of beech. While tough enough to stand up to heavy use, it should also be well finished in order not to damage any work or tools that are placed on it. Such a piece of equipment will have a solid top, sturdy legs, built-in vise, and probably a drawer or slots for holding tools. For those with limited space, there are now a number of small workbenches on the market,

either of wood or metal construction. These have most of the facilities offered by the traditional workbench, but with the added advantage that they can be folded up and stored away after use. This will probably be what most new woodworkers will buy. It will certainly enable you to cope admirably with all the projects that follow.

The basic tool kit

Brace
The brace or bit brace drill is the basic carpenter's drill. Together with the bits (drills), it can be used for boring and drilling most holes in wood. It involves much harder work than using a power drill and will tend to be less accurate. However, it will usually be considerably less expensive than a power drill and therefore initially what might be preferred. However, if you intend to do a lot of drilling and particularly if you want to drill into stone or brick, it would certainly be wise to consider buying a power drill.

Chisels
Chisels come in many and varied sizes. There are two basic types: the firmer chisels, which have blades of rectangular cross-section and are stronger and therefore better-suited to heavier work, and the bevel-edge chisels, which will do most chiseling jobs and also have the advantage of enabling you to get into tight corners because of their tapered edges. The most useful sizes tend to be ¼", ½", and 1". But whichever chisels you decide to buy, try to find those with unbreakable plastic handles rather than wooden ones.

C-clamp
This is the most useful gripping tool after the vise, and can be used for holding wood down as you saw, when you drill or mark out wood, and for holding pieces together while they are being glued.

The most useful sizes are from 2" to 8" (these are the maximum usable opening measurements, smaller sizes closing completely when screwed down). It is well worth having at least two clamps, one of 4" and the other of 8" maximum opening.

Be careful to tighten a C-clamp only with your hand and not with a tool such as a wrench, as this might bend the tool and will also cause dents in the surface of the wood being gripped. As a precaution, always place a spare piece of wood between the piece on which you are working and the clamp jaws to avoid such denting.

Gimlet
Resembling a corkscrew, the gimlet is used for making a starting hole for screws. It is turned in a clockwise direction to sufficient depth to enable the screw to bite into the wood. When removed, there will be a

protruding rim of wood on the surface that should be removed with sandpaper.

Hammer

Woodworking hammers are of two basic types, the *ball-pein* and the *claw*. The claw is the best general purpose hammer as it will both drive in and pull out most nails. When purchasing a claw hammer, make sure that the cut-away section of the claw tapers to a fine V-shape so that even the smallest pins can be extracted. The ball-pein is most useful for small nails and tacks, as well as for general-purpose work. As with all tools, quality and balance are important, and a good test of this with a claw hammer is to stand it upright on the claw where you should find it should remain.

Miter box

A miter box is an invaluable aid to cutting wood at an angle. It is essential for a neatly butting angle joint, such as may be required for a picture frame. Always be sure to use the miter box with a vise so that one hand is left free to hold steady the piece of wood that is being cut.

Power drill

Power tools take a lot of the hard work out of many jobs, and by far the most common is the electric drill. This comes with either single or variable speed motors, and the price you pay will reflect the size and capabilities of the equipment. The smaller, single-speed drills are now relatively inexpensive, and can cope with almost all woodworking tasks. Twist drill bits can be purchased in varying sizes, as can special bits for countersinking screws and spade bits for large diameter holes.

Saws

Coping saw

The coping saw is particularly useful for cutting curves, but will also cut practically any shape you require. Take care only to saw as far into the wood as the distance between the top of the saw and the blade. Cutting can start and finish at the edge of the wood or may be enclosed. Where an enclosed cut is required, first drill a hole in the waste part of the wood (that is, the part that you are going to cut out) and then feed the blade through the hole. Fix it into the frame of the saw, and then cut the shape you require. For the best result, make the cut in one complete operation rather than stopping halfway and starting the curve again from the other end.

Dovetail saw

This type of saw has a rigid back which makes it ideal for cutting joints accurately. The best saws will have around fifteen teeth per inch, which will ensure a fine cut.

Hand saw

This is the best kind of general-purpose saw as it will cut both with the grain and across it. The ideal length is about 24″ with around ten teeth per inch. It is best suited to cutting larger sheets or panels.

Jigsaw

Just as the power drill has virtually replaced the brace and bit, so too has the jigsaw come to be used as an alternative to the coping saw. It can accomplish all cutting jobs along a curved line with much greater accuracy and ease. It can also be used for cutting straight lines. You may, however, find it quite difficult to maintain an absolutely straight edge and prefer a conventional hand saw for such jobs.

Metal saw

The metal or hacksaw blade cuts only in one direction, forward. The blade is held in tension, and it will tend to stretch slightly after the first few cuts, after which it should be tightened up. Smaller hacksaws without a tensioning nut are also made, but these are really suitable only for very light work.

Screwdrivers

These are probably the most familiar tools in any house, but are also likely to be the most abused. You will need several sizes. Always make sure that you are using one in which the end fits exactly into the slot of the screw head. If the blade is too wide, it will damage the wood as you screw in; if the blade is too narrow or has become rounded at the end, it will chew up the slot of the screw. When using a screwdriver, always keep the blade absolutely square in the slot until the screw is driven home.

Square

This tool is used for squaring timber and for marking right angles for cutting. It is therefore essential for precision work and a good finish. As such, the angle should be checked for accuracy regularly. This can be done quite simply by laying the square along a straight edge, drawing a line down the blade and then turning the square over. If the square is accurate, the line of the blade will coincide.

Surform plane

The surform plane is a very inexpensive plane that facilitates the rapid stripping of wood but that is neither as accurate nor as smooth as the conventional and more expensive wood or metal plane.

Where a very smooth surface is required, care should be taken to hold the plane in line with the wood so that the teeth, set at 20 degrees to the body of the plane, will be cutting at an angle, giving a much smoother surface. Where the plane is held at an angle to the wood, the teeth will meet the grain square on. This will mean that the wood is cut much more quickly and more deeply.

Woodworking tips

To prevent a hammer head from slipping
If you use sandpaper to rub the head of a hammer from time to time, this should prevent it from becoming smooth. A smooth hammer head may easily slip when you are nailing, and may mark the wood with which you are working.

To hold nails in position when hammering
It is sometimes helpful to push nails through a piece of thick paper or card when hammering. The paper or card can easily be removed afterwards.

When using a power saw to cut timber
Do not use your hands to move the timber when using a power saw. This can be very dangerous. It will be safest to use a spare piece of wood to push the timber.

To avoid severing a power tool lead
When using a power tool, keep the lead over your shoulder. This will keep it safely out of the way.

When using an extension lead
You should never use a tool from an extension lead that is wound around a reel for longer than a few minutes. This will prevent overheating. Better still, unwind all the cable.

When transporting large pieces of wood
You can transport large sheets of wood most easily by means of a rope, which should measure twice as long as the wood. Tie it securely and hook it around the bottom corners of the wood. The wood can then be carried under your arm, as you hold the center of the rope.

When you use a cutting tool
For the sake of safety, keep the hand that is holding the wood *behind* the cutting tool.

When using a miter
It is helpful to have a vice for use with a miter box so that you have a free hand.

When tightening a C-clamp
It is wise only to tighten a C-clamp by hand. If you use a wrench, you may damage the surface of the wood by turning the C-clamp too tightly.

When filling the hole above a countersunk screw
In order to obtain the same color finish if the item is not to be painted, use sawdust from the same piece of wood, mixed with wood glue, to fill the holes above any countersunk screws.

Choosing wood

Wood is pleasurable to work with, and its excellent qualities should yield pleasing results. It is strong and lasting, yet fairly simple to cut and shape, and most people find its 'natural' appearance a refreshingly attractive alternative to plastic and other man-made materials.

For craft purposes, woods can be divided into two principal categories. *Hardwoods* consist mainly of woods from broadleaved trees – oak, mahogany and teak, for instance. *Softwoods*, meanwhile, come from coniferous trees, such as pine and larch.

Depending upon local facilities, you will be able to buy wood either from a 'do-it-yourself' shop, or from a timber yard. Whenever you can, it will be wise to get pieces cut to as near in length as possible to your final requirement, both to facilitate transport and to make your cutting tasks that much more simple. Both hard and softwoods are used to make plywood, which comprises veneers which are glued together. Plywood sheets vary in the number of veneers of which they made up: and the more sheets there are, the stronger the wood.

Keep a look-out, too, for old timber. Providing it is in good condition, there is no reason why it should not be recycled. Simply remove any nails or screws, and strip off any paint or varnish, and the wood will be ready for reuse in another form.

Nails and screws

Usually pre-packaged or purchased by weight, nails may be made of various substances, including brass, copper and steel, or they may be galvanized. There are also various type of nail, some particularly suited to the woodworking projects that follow. The *finishing nail* (also known as a *finishing brad*) is particularly useful for work where the nail has to be sunk. Its use will also help prevent the splitting of wood. For heavy work, you might seek *annular nails* which are useful for fixing plywood to other wood. Smaller finishing brads are essential when it comes to fixing thin plywood, or for other light nailing.

You will find that screws are sold by the gauge of their shanks and their length. They are usually made of steel, but can be obtained in brass which is preferable for outdoor items. For the projects that follow, you will need *flathead screws*, which can be inserted so that the head is either flush with the surface or below it. If inserted below, the gap can then be filled with plastic wood, which renders the screw invisible. *Round-headed screws* are usually called for when fixing metal to timber, or to provide a support, as with the chalkboard and easel, which you will find featured on page 54.

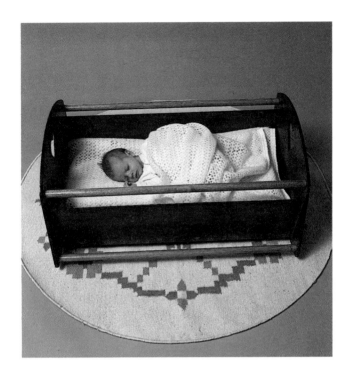

Rocking Cradle

What finer gift to make for a new baby than his or her very first cradle! This beautiful item based on a traditional American design could well become a family heirloom, after a child has perhaps in turn used it for dolls. Check that the mattress fits perfectly, and remember not to use a pillow for a small baby for fear of suffocation. Your infant should sleep soundly, soothed now and then by gentle rocking.

Materials
- 48" x 48" of ³⁄₈" plywood
- 12' of 1" diameter dowel
- 8' of 1" x 2" softwood (actual size ³⁄₄" x 1½")
- 40 No.4 x 1" screws

Tools
- plane saw
- jigsaw or coping saw
- screwdriver
- rasp or wood file
- drill with 2" hole saw attachment, ½" bit, and No.4 x 1" pilot bit.
- homemade compass, with thread, pencil, and nail

Cutting instructions
- bottom (from ³⁄₈" plywood): 31" x 16"
- sides (from ³⁄₈" plywood): 31" x 9" (2)
- ends (from ³⁄₈" plywood): 24" x 17" (2)
- lifting/rocking bars (from 1" diameter dowel): 33" (4)
- support battens (from 1" x 2" softwood): 16" (2) and 29½" (2)

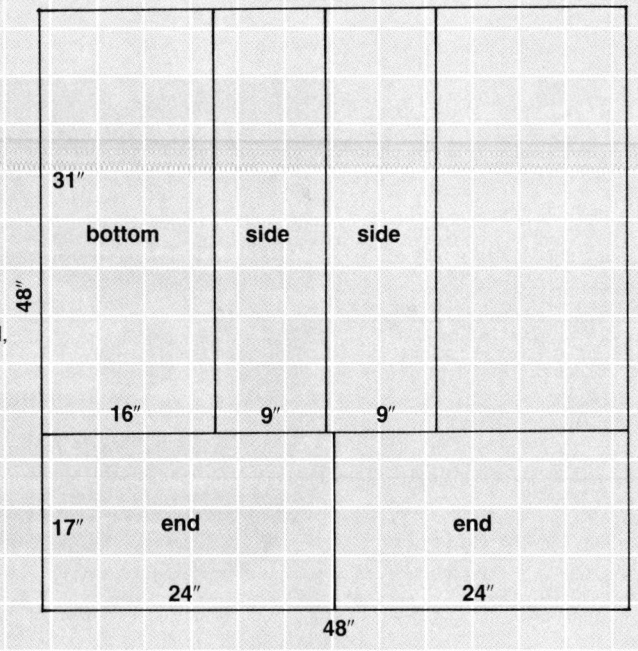

31"			
	bottom	**side**	**side**
48"			
	16"	**9"**	**9"**
17"	**end**		**end**
	24"		**24"**
		48"	

CUTTING DIAGRAM

Construction

1. Take one of the 17" x 24" end pieces, and draw a center line at 12". Mark points at 2¼", 3", 10", and 12½" from the base line (that is the 24" edge), and rule horizontal lines at these points.

2. On the 3" horizontal line and at a distance of 8" on either side of the center line, mark a point (*b*). Then on the 12½" horizontal line and at a point 10" on either side of the center line, mark (*a*). Connect points *a* and *b* on which line will lie the inside of the cradle sides.

3. From the point at which the center line meets the base (*c*), and using the homemade compass, describe an arc with a radius to *a*. This will give the shape to the top side. Lay the piece flat on the floor, and from a point projected 78" up from point *c* along the center line, describe another arc with a radius of 78". This will give the shape of the rockers, and only needs to be drawn as far as point *d*, as shown in the diagram. Draw a line connecting points *a* with points *d*. Cut out waste material to give the basic shape of the end piece.

4. Mark the position of the cradle side, noting that the top edge of the side comes to the point where the 10" horizontal cuts the line drawn between *a* and *b*. Measure 9" down from this point along the line between *a* and *b* and to a thickness of ³⁄₈". Mark three screw holes on the end panel in the center of this line. Repeat for the second side. Mark four further holes along the 2¼" horizontal line and at equal distances. This is where the bottom support battens will be fastened. At the same time, on the cradle sides, mark holes with a center at ³⁄₄" from the bottom edge and at intervals of approximately 4". Drill out and countersink all marked holes to take No.4 screws. (Note that the holes in the end pieces should be countersunk from the side opposite the markings – that is, the outside.)

5. Mark the dowel holes as shown in the diagram, with centers at a point 1¼" from each side in each

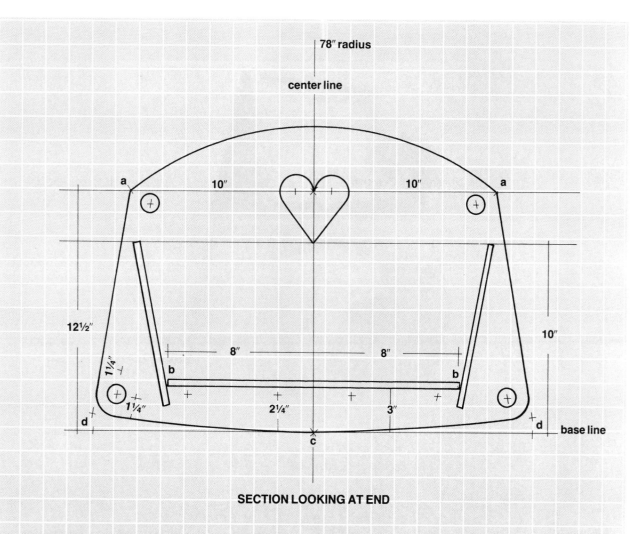

78″ radius

center line

a ⊕ 10″ 10″ ⊕ a

12½″

10″

1¼″

b 8″ 8″ b

1¼″ 2¼″ 3″

⊕ + + + + + + ⊕

d c d base line

SECTION LOOKING AT END

corner. Now round off the sharp corners as shown in the diagram.

6. If you wish to make a heart-shaped decoration at the end, cut two 2″ circles using the 2″ hole saw with centers on the 12½″ horizontal line and at an equal distance from the center line. Using a jigsaw, extend the circles with straight lines to a point at which the 10″ horizontal line crosses the center line. Smooth all edges.

7. Using a ½″ bit, drill about twenty ventilation holes all over the bottom and at a distance of 1½″ from each edge at intervals of 4″. Drill and countersink clearance holes for No.4 screws, through which the bottom will be fastened to the support battens.

8. Take the two end support battens, cut at angle to lines *a–b*, and glue and screw these through the pre-drilled holes centrally so that the top edge is on the 3″ horizontal line.

9. Get some help to position the sides onto the ends using the marks you have made. Glue and screw these into place through the pre-drilled holes. Drop in the bottom and screw onto the end support battens.

10. Fit the two long support battens under the base along the sides, and glue and screw them firstly through the pre-drilled holes on the sides and then through the bottom.

11. Round off the ends of the dowels and smooth with sandpaper. Fit through the holes in the end pieces and glue into position to make carrying handles and foot rockers.

12. Sand smooth with sandpaper and paint or stain as desired. Furnish with a foam mattress, 30″ x 16″ x 2″.

Chalkboard and Artist's Easel

Encourage a budding Picasso with this excellent playroom item that serves a dual purpose. One side has been designed to feature a chalkboard—a wonderful teaching accessory and also an excellent surface on which your child can draw with chalk. The other side offers the child the opportunity to paint on paper clipped to an easel like a true artist rather than having to draw on a horizontal surface. Why not make an artist's palette, too, with some leftover wood? Don't be too disappointed if you cannot recognize the subject matter of the junior masterpieces at first. Instead encourage your child to tell you all about his or her drawings, and display them in the kitchen or living room from time to time. Maximize your child's creative ability. Coloring books are all very well, but it can be rather restricting for a child always to be told to keep within the outlines.

Materials
- 3' x 2' of ¼" plywood
- 18' of 1" x 2" softwood (actual size ¾" x 1½")
- 6' of ⅜" x 1⅜" pine stop
- small pack of ¾" finishing nails
- 2 x 3" butt hinges
- 4 No.8 x 1" roundhead screws
- wood glue and sufficient screws for hinges

Tools
- dovetail saw
- hammer
- screwdriver
- drill with bits

Cutting instructions
- front and back boards (from ¼" plywood): (2) – A
  18" x 18"
- paint shelf (from ¼" plywood):- B
  18" x 3½"
- side brackets (from ¼" plywood): (2) – C
  2½" x 3½"
- side stays (from ¼" plywood): (2) – D
  11" x 2"
- legs (from 1" x 2" softwood): (4) – E
  36"
- frame (from 1" x 2" softwood): (4) – F
  16½"
- shelf fronts (from ⅜" x 1⅜" pine stop): (2) – G
  18"

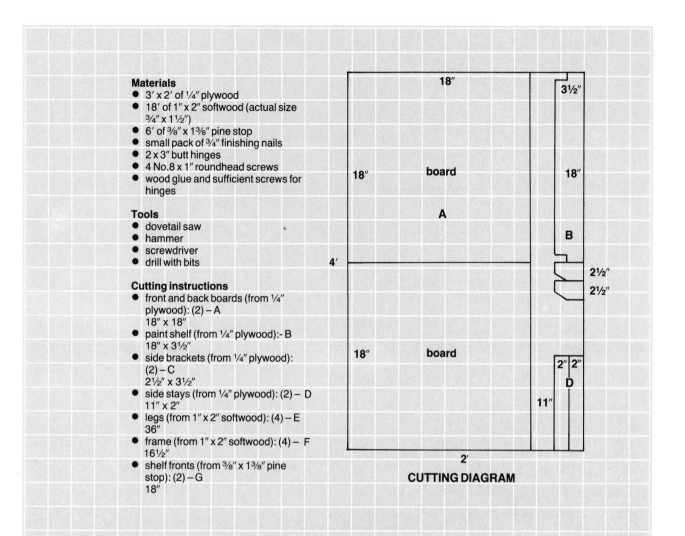

CUTTING DIAGRAM

Construction

1. With nails and glue attach the plywood boards (A) to the four legs (E) flush at top end. Glue and nail the horizontal frame pieces (F) between the legs. Note that the frame is on the outside. With the two plywood surfaces uppermost and the tops end to end, fix two 3" butt hinges flat onto the plywood at a distance of 2" from each side.

2. Take the paint shelf (B) and cut out a retangle ¾" x 1½" from two corners so that it can slot in on top of the lower horizontal frame piece. Glue and nail a length of ⅜" x 1⅜" pine stop to the front edge, and glue and nail the shelf into position. Next, shape the side brackets (C) as in the diagram and glue and nail into shape, supporting the shelf at either end on the outside of the frame.

3. Take another length of ⅜" x 1⅜" pine stop and fasten this to the bottom rail on the other frame piece to make a shelf for chalk pieces.

4. Shape the two side stays as shown in the diagram, and drill holes centrally ¾" from each end to clear size 8 screws. Cut a slot to the hole at one end of each stay. With the roundhead screws, screw through the other end into the easel leg, 22" from the top of the chalkboard. Screw in the other screws 22" from the top on the other leg. Do not screw in fully, but leave sufficient distance between the screw head and the leg to enable the stay to engage.

5. Sand smooth. Paint the chalkboard side with four or five coats of paint. Stain and varnish the frame and painting side. Add a hook or fasten a bulldog clip through the painting side to hold paper. Alternatively, use drawing pins.

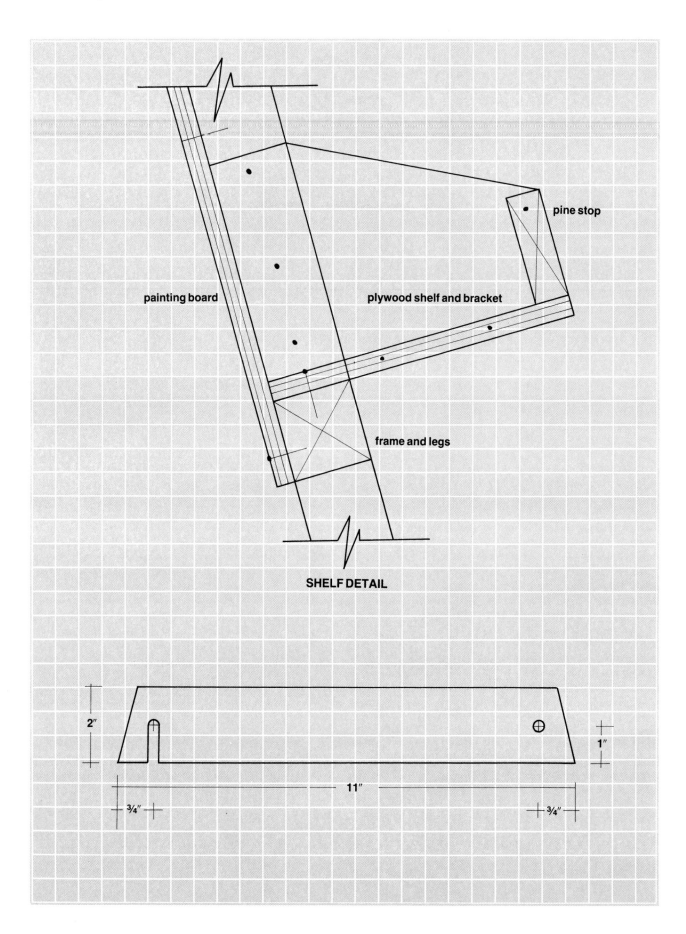

pine stop

painting board

plywood shelf and bracket

frame and legs

SHELF DETAIL

2″

1″

11″

¾″

¾″

Portable Highchair

Soon after weaning begins, it will be an excellent idea for your child to join you for meals—not sitting at the table but in his or her very own highchair. Most commercially produced highchairs are somewhat impractical. This model, however, is readily portable, can be taken apart, and is easily reassembled. It is therefore ideal for taking along in the car when visiting friends or relatives for the day, or when on a family vacation. As always where children's furniture is concerned, stability is a vital factor. Notice the broad base. The design is delightfully nostalgic in appeal, and has something of the art deco period about it. Falling out of a highchair is a very common accident. We recommend that an infant not be left on his or her own even when in the chair, nor should a child be left in the chair for very long periods so that movement is unnecessarily restricted.

Materials
- 48″ x 50″ of ½″ plywood
- 6′ of ¾″ x ¾″ hardwood
- 36″ of 1″ x ⅛″ veneer plywood
- 12″ of ¾″ diameter dowel
- 15 No.6 x 1″ brass flathead screws
- pack of ½″ nails
- hook and eye

Tools
- plane saw
- jigsaw/coping saw
- drill with ¾″ bit
- screwdriver
- hammer
- homemade compass with thread, pencil, and nail

Cutting instructions
all in ½″ plywood
- sides: 33½″ x 21″ (2)
- base: 19″ x 6″ (2)
- seat: 14″ c 13″
- back: 16½″ x 15″
- table: 16½″ x 13″

Construction

1. Draw a vertical center line on the short side (21″) of one of the side pieces, and a horizontal line from a point 28¾″ from the bottom of the piece.

2. The trimmed width is 20½″ at the base and 13½″ at the top. Draw up as shown in the diagram, describing an arc with a radius of 4½″ and its center at a point 2½″ to the rear of the vertical center line and on the horizontal line.

3. Drill a ¾″ hole with its center ¾″ from each edge at the top and front of the side.

4. Mark a point along the horizontal line, 4½″ to the rear of the vertical center line and another point 4″ up the vertical center line from the base of the side. Mark out a slot ½″ wide along the line connecting these two points. The slot should extend from the top edge to a point 2″ below the horizontal line. The back of the chair will be located into this slot.

5. Mark another cut-out for the seat. This should be at a distance of 22¾″ from the bottom edge of the side piece, and should be 5½″ long and ½″ wide.

6. From the bottom edge of each side piece, mark out a slot 3″ long and ½″ wide along the vertical center line. Draw a horizontal line 1¼″ from the bottom edge to a point 2″ from either end. When this piece is cut out, make sure that the edges are rounded off as shown in the diagram.

7. Mark the position of the hardwood support battens.

8. Cut out all the marked-off areas on the side piece.

9. Repeat for the second side.

10. On the table piece, draw a vertical center line in the middle of the 16½″ side. From a point 4″ up from the base and along the vertical center line, draw a circle with a radius of 8″. From a point projected along the vertical center line 10″ below the first radius point (that is, 6″ from the bottom edge of the piece), make a second radius of 8″ and mark up as shown in the diagram.

11. Drill and countersink four holes to take size 6 screws for locating the ¾″ x ¾″ arms at 6⅜″ from the center line. There should be two holes on each side.

12. Cut out the table with a jigsaw. Smooth all the edges.

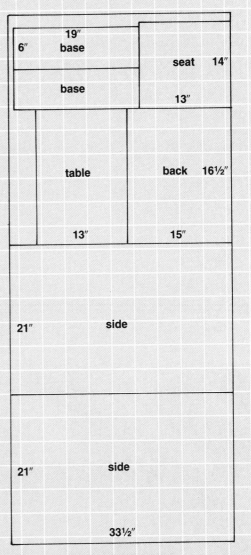

CUTTING DIAGRAM

13. On the back piece, draw a vertical center line in the middle of the 16½″ side. Then draw a circle with a radius of 8″, and the center at a point projected 6″ from the base line along the vertical center line.

14. Mark out slots for locating the back into the side pieces. These should be 5½″ from either side of the center line, to a distance of 6″ (that is, ½″ wide) and to a depth of 5⅛″ from the bottom edge.

15. Mark out the back to a point 2″ on either side of the vertical center line and to a depth of 1½″ from the bottom edge. Draw a horizontal line from these two points to leave a 4″ tongue in the center of the back, which will slot into the seat. Cut out all the marked pieces.

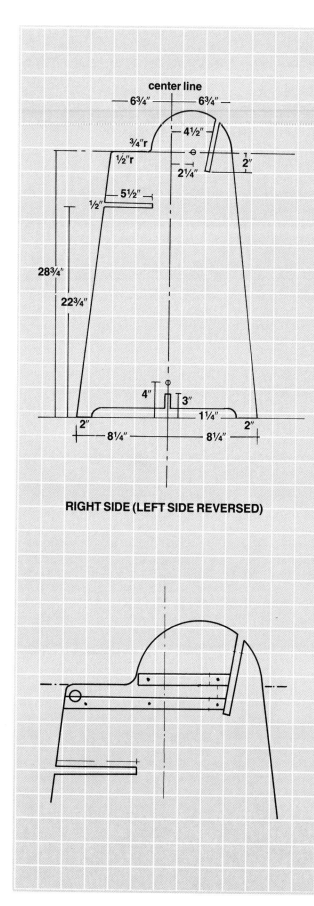

center line

— 6¾" — | — 6¾" —

— 4½" —

¾"r

½"r

2¼"

2"

5½"

½"

28¾"

22¾"

4"

3"

1¼"

2"

8¼"

8¼"

2"

RIGHT SIDE (LEFT SIDE REVERSED)

16. Draw a vertical center line from the middle of the 14″ side of the seat piece and mark two points at 5½″ on either side of this on one side. Draw vertical lines 7¼″ long from both these points. Mark out two more lines parallel to these at a distance of 6″ from the vertical center line.

17. Draw a horizontal line from the base line to show the position of the two slots. Cut away the marked-off areas. Now mark out a slot ⅝″ wide, in which to locate the back of the chair, at a distance of 10⅝″ from the front of the seat and 2″ either side of the vertical center line.

18. Draw a vertical center line from the 19″ side of the base piece and 3″ from the top. Mark points 6″ and 6½″ on either side. Mark two more points along the top edge at 5⅞″ and 6⅜″ from the vertical center line. Join up these points to make the angled slots into which the sides will be located. Mark a cut-out 7½″ either side of the vertical center line and 1¼″ deep.

19. Now assemble the chair: first the seat and sides, then the back, which slots through the seat, followed by the 12″ x ¾″ diameter dowel. Next, slot in the base, noting that the sides need to be pushed outwards to create tension and thereby extra stability. File or sand slots if necessary.

20. With the chair standing on the floor and the two table arms in place between the side battens, position the table so that the back edge is 3¼″ from the side vertical center line. Now screw battens into place, checking that it slides in and out smoothly. Finish the table by gluing and nailing the 1″ x ⅛″ plywood strip around the outer edge in order to create a lip.

21. Sand smooth all rough edges and fill any holes. Before painting or varnishing, remove the battens and treat with teak oil. Avoid painting table arms and treat in the same way to ensure a smooth fit. Fit a hook and eye between the side and the table arm to prevent the table from sliding out.

22. The dowel prevents the baby from slipping out when the tray is removed. However, for very small children, it may be advisable to make a strip to fasten around the dowel and under the seat to prevent the child from slipping under the dowel. Holes can also be drilled in the sides for fitting a harness.

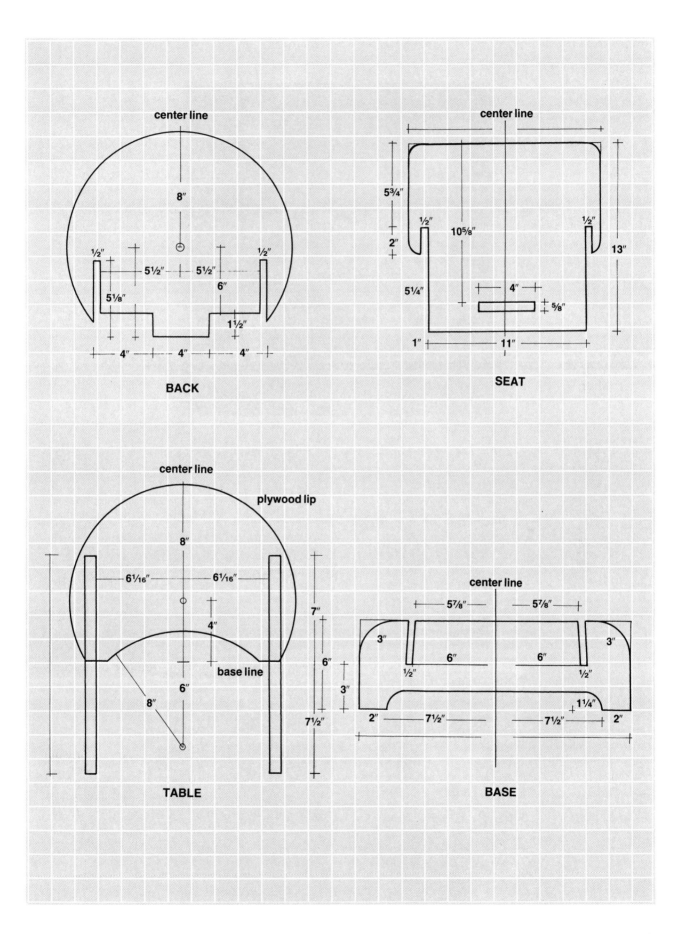

Rocking Horse

Traditionally, the rocking horse is a firm childhood favorite. Antique models sometimes fetch a fortune, and modern rocking horses can be very expensive too. They are certainly attractive in appearance and may even feature as part of the living room decor. But small children often find them frightening, sometimes because they rock rather violently and sometimes because toddlers feel unsafe when far from the ground. This small rocking horse will delight any young child, and should be quite safe if well constructed. There is also a small storage area at the rear so that your child can take along a few toys when riding off on a pretend journey. Paint or stain the horse, as you prefer, but if you are not confident about painting his coat, perhaps decorate the piebald horse with stick-on circles, as shown here.

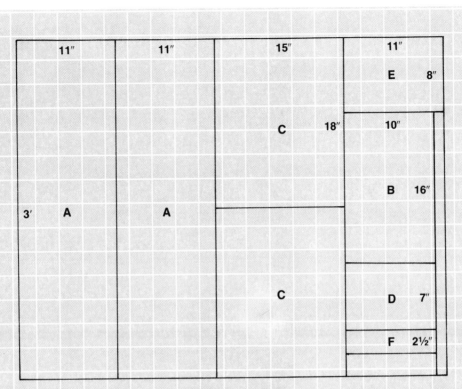

CUTTING DIAGRAM

Materials
- 4′ x 3′ of ½″ plywood, A–D interior, or better
- 8″ of ¾″ diameter dowel
- 40 No.6 x 1¼″ wood screws
- wood glue

Tools
- hand saw
- electric jigsaw/coping saw
- drill
- C-clamps
- chisel
- wood rasp or file
- homemade compass with string, nail, and pencil

Cutting instructions
all in ½″ plywood
- sides: 36″ x 11″ (2) – A
- foot rest: 16″ x 10″ – B
- head: 18″ x 15″ (2) – C
- center: 10″ x 7″ – D
- seat: 11″ x 8″ – E
- back: 10″ x 2½″ – F

Construction

1. Cut out all the pieces. Glue the two head pieces (C) together, and use C-clamps or heavy weights to make firm bonding. It is important to get a good right angle in the bottom right hand corner as measurements will be taken from this point.

2. Place a side piece (A) on a large flat surface and draw a vertical line at a distance of 14½″ from the left-hand end of the long edge from which subsequent measurements will be taken. Using the homemade compass, with its center at a point 40″ from the bottom of the piece along the vertical line, describe an arc on (A).

3. Measure a distance of 14″ to the left and 18″ to the right of the vertical line. From these points, draw another vertical line. Points (P) and (Q) respectively are at the point where these lines cross the arc previously drawn. Now measure 1¼″ above and ⅞″ below points (P) and (Q) on a line at 90° to the arc (that is, on its radius) and draw a tangent from the arc to the lower mark at either end, as shown in the diagram.

4. Mark a point 6″ up from the bottom edge of (A) and 2″ to the front of the center line: this is point (R). Mark a further point 8″ up the center line and 10⅝″ to the rear: this is point (S). Along the top edge of (A), make another mark 8″ from the vertical line: this is point (T). Now join up all these points as shown in the diagram and cut out, rounding all corners and sharp angles, except the one at which the seat will be fitted.

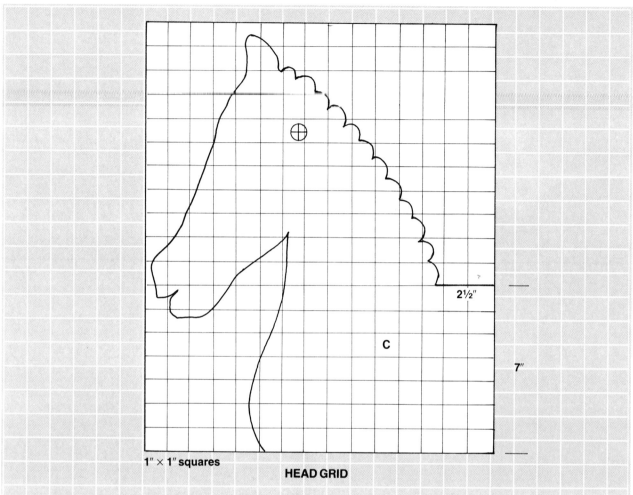

1" × 1" squares

HEAD GRID

5. Mark out the positions of pieces (B), (D), and (F), as shown in the diagram, taking note that the front edge of (D) should be 3" from the vertical line, and at the top edge of (B) is 7" from the top edge of (A), extending 6½" to the front of the vertical line. Take special care that pieces (B), (D), and (F) are all set at right angles to each other. Mark out screw holes as shown in the diagram.

6. On the seat piece (E), mark a cut-out ½" deep and 1" wide in the center of the 11" width. Cut this out with a saw and chisel. The horse's head will fit into this slot.

7. On piece (B) mark a vertical line midway on the shortest side for screwing and positioning the head. Mark another line along the longest edge at a point 9¾" from the front for drilling screw holes for fixing (B) to (D). Mark three holes at equal distances along this line. Also mark piece (F) for these screws at ¼" from the bottom edge for fastening to (B).

8. Drill and countersink all holes for size 6 screws. Note that sides (A) should be countersunk from the opposite side to the marks. If the appearance of

rounded projections on the surface is not objectionable, use roundhead screws to eliminate countersinking.

9. After getting some help to hold the pieces in place, glue and screw (B) to (D), and then (F) to (B). Then fix this assembly to the sides (A) and finally fix the seat (E) in position.

10. When the bonded pieces (C) have dried, mark up a 1" grid starting in the bottom right hand corner. Copy the head in the illustration, and mark the handle point. Cut out using a jigsaw, and smooth with a rasp and medium sandpaper. Finally, drill a ¾" hole for the handles (drill from both sides with a spade bit to avoid splintering) and then cut an 8" length of ¾" dowel. Round off the ends, and fit and glue centrally.

11. Insert the head into the body, and glue and screw in place. For extra strength, screw through the center of (D) into the back of (C).

12. Fill all screw holes and finish in paint, or stain and varnish.

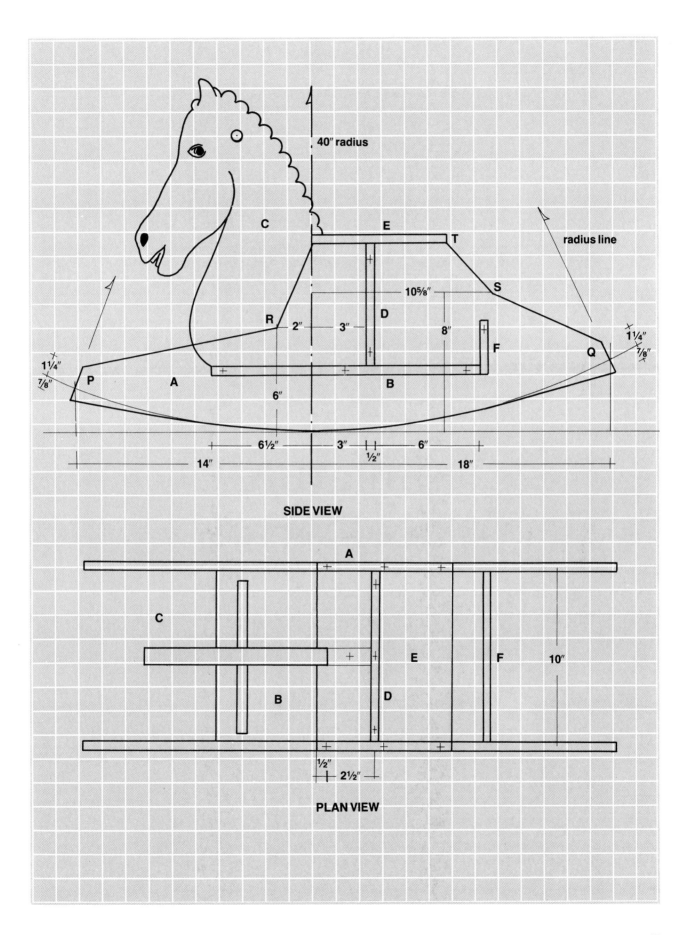

SIDE VIEW

PLAN VIEW

Miniature Wheelbarrow

Small children love helping in the garden, and will particularly welcome a plot of their own. See that it is as colorful as possible, and that there is something of interest in it all year round. How wonderful for them to have a few personal tools, too! This miniature wheelbarrow is not only charming, it will also be useful to a toddler for collecting stones or when picking weeds. Your child may also find it a convenient way of transporting toys both in and around the garden.

Materials

- 4' x 1½' of ½" plywood, exterior grade
- 7' of 1" x 3" softwood (actual size ¾" x 2½")
- 7¼" of 1" diameter dowel
- 4 No.8 x 1½" brass screws
- 10 No.8 x 1¼" brass screws
- 20 No.6 x 1" brass screws
- pack of 1" brads
- waterproof wood glue

Tools

- jigsaw
- drill with bits
- screwdriver
- hammer
- rasp or wood file

Cutting instructions

all from ½" plywood
- sides: 7" x 17": (2) – A
- back: 7" x 10" – B
- front: 10" x 10" – C
- base: 9" x 9" – D
- wheels: circle, 8" diameter (3) – E
  See construction notes for cutting method

Construction

1. To make sides (A), mark out a rectangle 9" x 7" high. On the top extend the line by 1" on one side and by 7" on the other. Join these points to the base corners and cut out.

2. To make the back (B), draw a rectangle 8" x 7" high. On the top side, extend the line 1" on both sides. Join both these points to the base corners and cut out.

3. To make the front (C), draw a rectangle 8" x 10" high. Extend the top line by 1" on either side. Join both these points to the base corners and cut out. Note that the front (C) needs a bevel planing at the bottom so that it will fit flush on the base and against the sides. This can be achieved by marking a line of the same thickness as the plywood up from the leading edge.

4. When the pieces have been cut, mark screw holes on piece (A), ¼" in from the front and back edges, three per side to fit No.6 screws. Now glue and screw the front and back pieces (C) and (B) to both sides. On the base (D), mark screw holes ¼" in from all the edges and drill for size 6 screws. Countersink the screw holes, glue, and screw the base onto the sides, front and back. Note that it might be necessary to plane the bottom of the sides to the base in order to ensure a good fit. Make sure, too, that all the top edges are flush.

5. To make the wheel struts, cut two lengths of 1" x 3", each 14" long. At one end, mark a point 2" in and ⁹⁄₁₆" up on the 2½" side of the wood. Drill through both pieces at this point, using a 1" drill bit. Take care to keep the holes as true as possible, as this will be the axle support. Saw off the two quarters of the circle on the edge to create a slot. Sand as required to allow the axle to turn freely.

6. Cut two more pieces of 1" x 3", each one 5½" long, for the legs. Glue and screw them, using 1¼" screws, to the other end of the wheel struts and at right angles. Next, fasten the struts/legs to the base of the wheelbarrow, gluing and screwing with 1¼" screws through the bottom having made holes on a line ⅝" from the inside edge of each side. Care should be taken that the legs come flush to the edge and that the two struts for holding the wheel are parallel.

7. Cut two pieces of 1" x 3", each one 14" long, to form the handles. Shape each at one end using a jigsaw, and then screw and glue to the sides flush with the top edge, 4" in from the back. Use screws as shown.

8. Using a jigsaw, cut the three circles (E). These can be rough cut at first, then glued and nailed together, making the final accurate cut through all three at once. When set, drill a 1" hole through the center and glue in a piece of 1" dowel, 7¼" long and fixed exactly in the center. Turn the wheelbarrow upside down and drop into the pre-cut slots. Cut two plates 1¼" x 2½", from scraps of plywood, and glue and nail these onto the outside of the wheel struts to hold the axle in place. Cut two bottom pieces, 1¼" x 2½", and screw these in underneath to hold the axle in place.

9. Sand down and either paint or, if to be left outside, treat with a wood preservative.

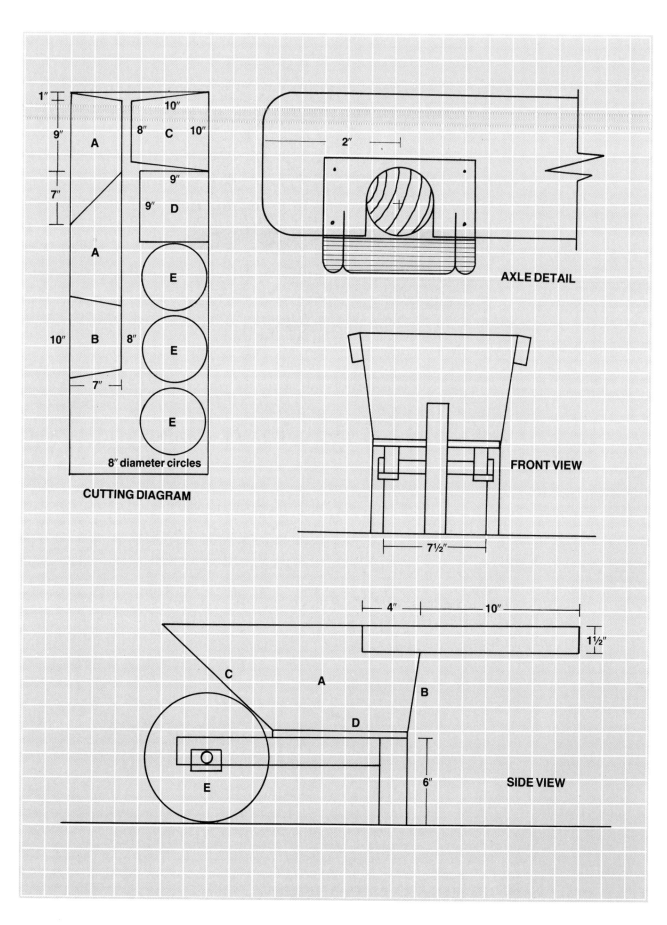

1″
9″
10″
8″ C 10″
A
7″
9″
9″ D
A
E
10″ B 8″
E
7″
E
8″ diameter circles

CUTTING DIAGRAM

2″

AXLE DETAIL

7½″

FRONT VIEW

4″ 10″
1½″
C
A
B
D
6″

SIDE VIEW

E

Building Blocks

As Dr. Spock put it, "A good size bag of wooden blocks of different shapes is worth ten toys to any child up to six or eight." These wooden blocks are suitable for babies from about nine months. Because of their extreme versatility, they fascinate adults, too. (In fact, why not make yourself a set as an adult toy!) They make a refreshing change from plastic bricks, and are quite lightweight. Blocks provide some of the most creative opportunities for small children. Initially, they may not seem as exciting as a model train, a car, or a space rocket, but with a little imagination they can be all these things on different days. The more blocks you make, the greater the potential.

Materials
● 9' of prepared 2" x 2" clear softwood is sufficient to make the illustrated set. Other square stock may be used if it is more available than the 2" x 2" stock.

Tools
● miter box with saw

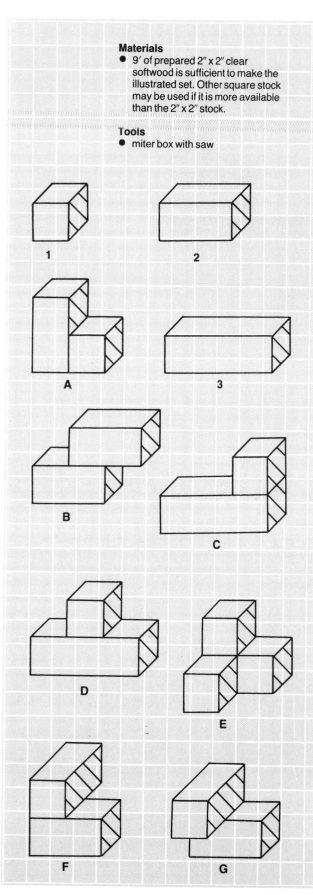

Construction
1. Check that the wood is reasonably square in section, and plane or sand smooth. Any planing done to achieve square stock is best done on a power jointer or by a lumberyard mill shop.

2. The blocks are made from pieces cut to three sizes only, as follows:
(i) a regular cube (use the width of a spare piece of 2" x 2" softwood to get length).
(ii) 2 cubes long (use two widths to get length).
(iii) 3 cubes long (use three widths to get length).
Accurate cutting is most important and will result in a good fitting set. Remember to sand down well all end grains.

3. Make up two of each of the shapes A–G, as illustrated. Apply a small amount of glue over one of the surfaces, but not on the end grain, and rub the blocks together on the joint until they feel sticky. Remove any excess glue with a damp cloth and leave to dry. Give a final sand down.

4. The most satisfactory finish is staining, followed by three coats of polyurethane varnish, diluting the first coat with equal parts of spirit. Try to avoid runs.

5. The set can be made into a variety of cubes or rectangular shaped blocks, or just stacked to make whatever shape you want. With imagination, you can construct a space rocket, a house, a car, or many other play objects. The possibilities are endless.

Dollhouse

A dollhouse is usually so expensive to buy, whether new or antique, that many small girls and boys, although they would dearly love one, miss out on the fun of playing with a miniature home. Even a very sophisticated model like this is, however, quite cheaply made. An ideal birthday or Christmas gift for a child of four years and over and one that even the fairly inexperienced woodworker should be able to complete in two or three weekends, the house presents tremendous opportunities for imaginative play. Note how the lid lifts to allow maximum light. You can either buy pieces of dollhouse furniture bit by bit, or make these, too, from matchboxes, cardboard, leftover wood, cork, felt, and scraps of fabric. Consider making a little sign for the house to display its name or number. You can even make little occupants from pipe-cleaners and clothespins.

Materials
- 4' x 3'4" of ⅜" plywood
- 40" of ½" x ¼" hardwood
- 40" of ¼" x ¼" hardwood
- 20" of ½" half-round
- 2" of ¼" half-round
- 20" of ¾" piano hinge
- 36" of ⅛" piano hinge
- small pack of ½" finishing nails
- 50 No.4 x ⅜" wood screws
- small piece of ¼" thick foam weatherstrip
- wood glue

Tools
- panel saw
- coping saw or electric jigsaw
- metal saw
- hammer
- power drill or brace with 1" bit
- ⅜" chisel
- plane or rasp
- gimlet

Cutting instructions
all from ⅜" plywood
- end walls and room divider: 8" x 20", sloping to 18" from center line (3) – A
- back wall: 17¾" x 19" – B
- roof: 5½" x 20" (2) – C
- base: 9½" x 20" – D
- upper floor: 8" x 18¼" – E
- front: 9½" 17½" (2) – F

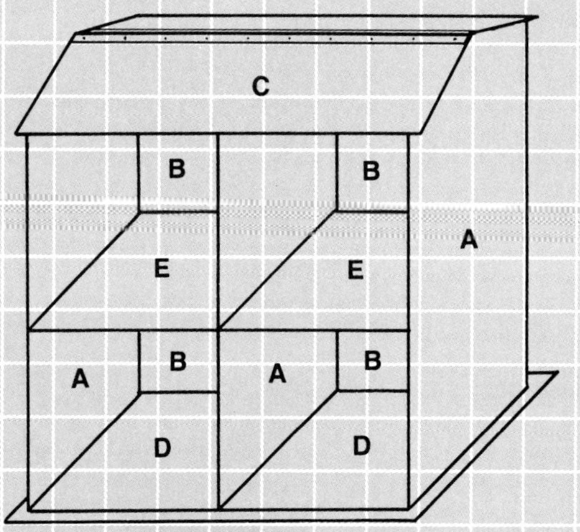

ISOMETRIC

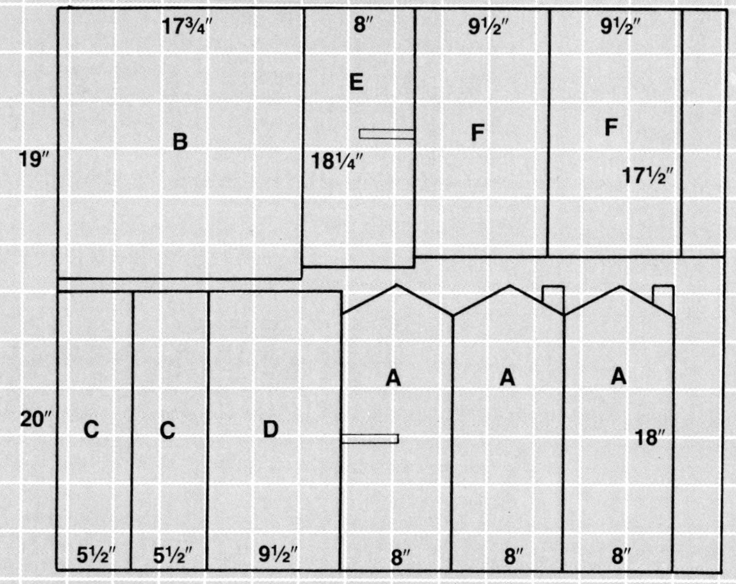

CUTTING DIAGRAM

Construction

1. Take the two end walls (A) and drill a 1" hole centrally in each, at a distance of 2" from the apex. These will act as handles.

2. From the center line of the room divider (A) mark out a slot ⅜" wide by 4" deep from the rear edge. Make a similar cut in the first floor (E), ⅜" wide by 4" deep from the front edge and midway along its length. These two pieces will now slot together to form the four rooms of the house.

3. Mark the center line at 9½" on the back (B) and make another mark at right angles to this at 9" from the bottom edge. Make similar marks at 9" on the two end walls (A).

4. With glue, hammer, and finishing nails, assemble the upper floor (E), the room divider (A), and then the two end walls (A). Next, glue and nail the whole assembly onto (B) along the lines marked, taking care to fix the four corners first, then the center. For a better grip, angle the nails.

5. Draw a center line on the base (D) and two more lines ½" from the back and sides. Glue and nail the walls along these lines. There will now be a border around the base of the house.

6. Place the roof pieces (C) on the slope of the walls and see how much has to be shaved off in order to make an apex. With the rasp or plane, take off a sufficient amount to allow a reasonable fit.

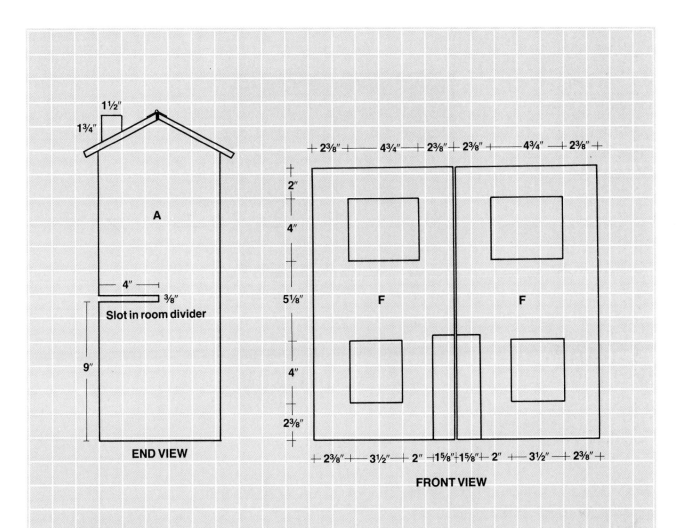

END VIEW

1½"

1¾"

A

4"

⅜"

Slot in room divider

9"

FRONT VIEW

2⅜"   4¾"   2⅜"   2⅜"   4¾"   2⅜"

2"

4"

5⅛"

4"

2⅜"

F   F

2⅜"   3½"   2"   1⅝" 1⅝"   2"   3½"   2⅜"

7. Mark a line ½" from each end of one roof piece (C) and then glue and nail onto the front slope along this line. Placing the other roof piece in position, attach the two together with the 20" strip of piano hinge, using the ⅜" screws. The roof will now lift up at the back and the hinge becomes the ridge tiles.

8. Mark up the windows. The two top windows measure 4¾" wide by 4" high and are set centrally in each front piece, 2" from the top edge. The two bottom windows are 3½" wide by 4" high and are set at a distance of 2⅜" from the outside edge, 2⅜" from the bottom. Cut out the window holes using a coping saw or electric jigsaw. Use the ¼" x ¼" hardwood to form a crosspiece in each window. Cut to make a tight fit and glue into place.

9. Use the ¼" half-round as window sills, making sure that these are ¼" longer than the window openings. Cut a door frame with mitred corners from the ½" half-round and screw in the two small cabinet knobs as front door handles on either side of the center opening. Note that the door is not cut out but indicated by the frame.

10. Using an offcut from piece A, cut two chimneys 4" long at an angle so that, when attached to the front sloping roof, they will act as a support for the lifting back section and also make a flat play surface. When correctly positioned, glue into place.

11. Attach the ½" piano hinges to the back of each front opening wall. Cut, glue, and nail with ½" nails two strips of ½" x ¼" hardwood along the leading edge of the side walls to act as a support for the hinges. Fasten the other side of the piano hinge to this piece using size 4 x ⅜" screws, and taking care to leave a 1/16" gap in the center. Use a short strip of foam weatherstrip on the room divider to cushion the doors and to hold the front flush.

12. Give a final rubdown with fine sandpaper. Stain or paint as desired.

Bird Feeder

Make this very attractive bird feeder as a special surprise. Not only will it provide a decorative element for the yard, it will also be an excellent way of encouraging your child's interest in those species of feathered wildlife to be found within the confines of his or her own environment. Check that you construct the table so that it is high enough to put off even the most determined cats. It is essential to treat the wood so that it is hardy enough to withstand all weathers. This applies below ground level, too, so that the wood will not rot. Have fun together with your children putting out nuts, bread, water, and scraps of suitable food for the birds either on the table or hanging in net or wire bags. The bird feeder also features drainage channels so that it will not flood in heavy rain.

Materials
- 32" x 16" of ⅜" plywood
- 8" of 2" x 2" softwood (actual size 1½" x 1½" minimum)
- 14" of ½" diameter dowel
- 5' of ¾" x ¾" pine quarter round
- 16 No.8 x 1" roundhead brass screws
- 16 No.4 x ¾" roundhead brass screws

Tools
- electric drill with bits
- screwdriver
- hand saw
- electric jigsaw/coping saw

Cutting instructions
all from ⅜" plywood
- table supports: 2 triangular pieces from a square, 8" x 8"
- roof supports: 2 triangular pieces from a square, 4" x 4"
- table: 11" x 16"
- roof piece: 8" x 6⅜"
- roof piece: 8" x 6"

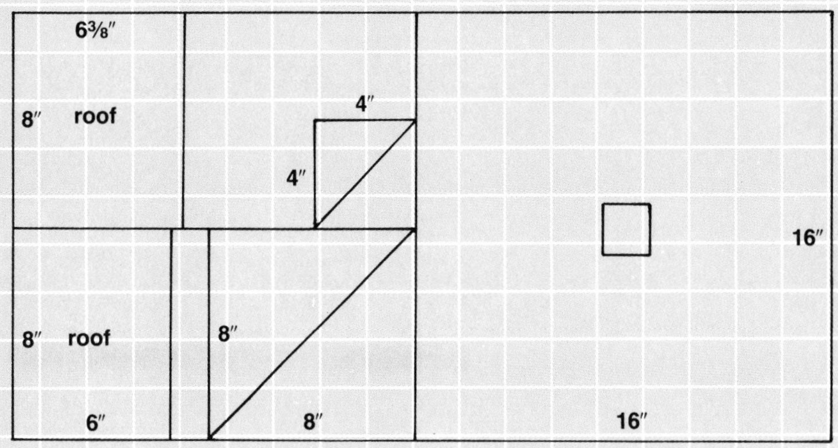

CUTTING DIAGRAM

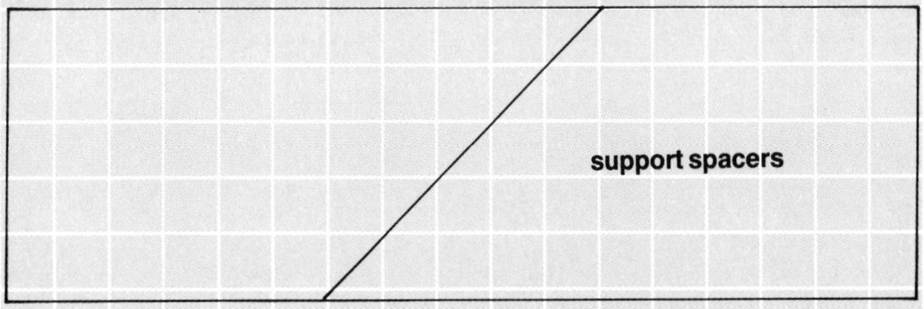

support spacers

Construction

1. Cut 7' from the piece of 2" x 2" softwood to make the post. At one end of the post, drill two ½" holes at right angles to each other, and at points 4" and 8" down from the top of the post.

2. From the remaining piece of 2" x 2" softwood, cut out two table support spacers, as shown in the diagram. Mark the triangular table supports for screw holes (see diagram). Drill for No.8 x 1" screws. Position one of the large triangles so that its apex is pointing downwards and its base is along a line 12"from the top of the post and at right angles to it. Screw into position firmly. Repeat for the second triangle, making sure that the two line up

exactly. Now slot in the two 2" x 2" spacers so that all edges are flush, and then screw together.

3. Drill holes for ¾" screws around the table edge, four on each side, and attach a 14" length of ¾" x ¾" quarter-round on each side, 1" in from the corners of the table to provide a gap at each corner for drainage. Saw off the 1" x 1" corners of the table on a diagonal line. Using the jigsaw, cut a square 2" x 2" in the center of the table.

4. Drill two holes in the table and above the support spacers to fit size 8 screws. Drop the table over the top of the post so that it rests on the support. Screw and fix in position.

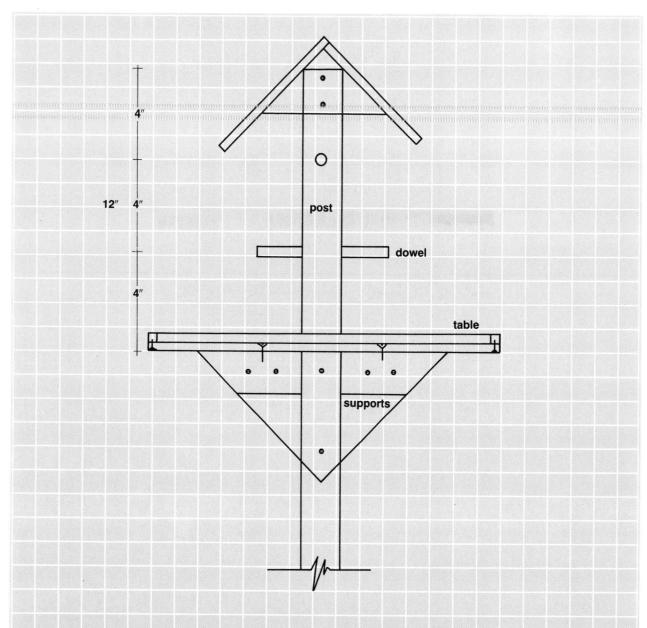

5. Drill and fix the smaller triangles in position at the top of the post and with their apexes pointing upwards (see diagrams).

6. Mark up the two roof sections that will be screwed onto the edge of the support triangles. Drill holes to take size 4 screws along a line parallel to and approximately $^{15}/_{16}''$ from a center line. There should be four screws per side, two into each support. Note that the wider roof piece overlaps the other at the top, making a flush finish.

7. Cut two lengths from the ½" dowel, one of 6" and one of 8". Hammer these into the previously drilled holes, the longer one at the top. (If the fit is not tight and gluing is necessary, be sure to use a water-resistant wood glue.)

8. Treat with a wood preservative and stain to blend in with the surroundings. It is best if the post can stand in a pot of preservative overnight. Add brass screw hooks as required for hanging bags of nuts and other bird foods.

9. Dig a hole 12"–14" deep, drop in the post, and fill in with soil, packing firmly with a heavy stick, a little at a time.

10. Stock the table with grains, seeds, nuts, and other tidbits. Don't forget water, too.

Teddy Bear
Bookends

A love for books is something that can and should be instilled in the home beginning with the preschool years. From only a few months old, babies will enjoy looking at the pictures in fabric or board books and delight at the turning of pages. These may get a bit tacky as the result of clumsy handling and sticky fingers, but once a child begins to learn to read, he or she can be taught that books should be treated with care. They also need to be readily accessible, and a set of attractive bookends like these will encourage your child to keep his or her books not only displayed with pride but also in good order.

Materials
- 24″ x 16″ of ½″ plywood
- 4″ of ⅜″ dowel
- 15 No.6 x 1″ screws

Tools
- hand saw
- electric jigsaw/coping saw
- drill with bits
- screwdriver
- C-clamp
- rasp or surform plane

Cutting instructions
all from ½″ plywood
- body: 9″ x 4″ (2) – A
- leg: 6″ x 2¼″ (4) – B
- arm: 4½″ x 1¾″ (4) – C
- back: 8″ x 6″ (2) – D
- Base: 6″ x 6″ (2) – E

Construction

1. Draw up a 1″ grid on tracing paper and, using this, mark out the teddy bear body, arms, and legs. Note that the body's back and base are not rounded but make a right angle.

2. Cut out all the pieces, if possible clamping two together for an even cut. Smooth off all edges first with a surform plane and then with smooth sandpaper.

3. Using a ⅜″ drill bit, drill dowel holes for the arms and legs in the position illustrated.

4. Cut four pieces of ⅜″ dowel, each 1½″ long, and glue these into the body so that equal amounts protrude on either side.

5. On the pre-cut base and back pieces, draw a center line at 3″, and on this mark screw holes to line up with the flat areas of the teddy bear back and base. Mark three holes at a distance of ¼″ from the bottom of the back piece for fixing to the base. Drill and countersink all holes to fit No.6 screws. Then glue and screw the back to the base.

6. Paint or stain and varnish all the pieces, drawing in eyes and mouth with indelible felt-tip pen.

7. When dry, assemble the body, arms, and legs (these should fit tightly onto the dowels) and screw to the back and base through the pre-drilled holes, making sure that the screws go in centrally.

8. To prevent slipping, put some felt on the base.

1″ × 1″ **grid**

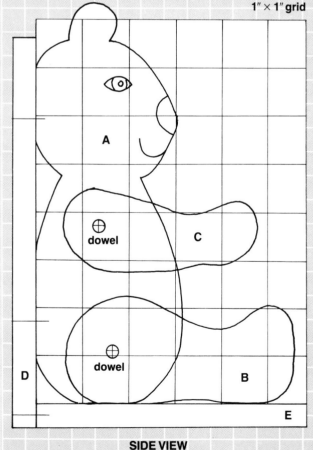

SIDE VIEW

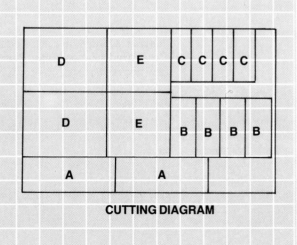

CUTTING DIAGRAM

Desk with Storage

Having a desk of his or her own will almost certainly encourage your child to get on with homework, as well as hobbies that require a flat surface. It will also help save the surface of your dining room table! A wide ridge has been incorporated into this design so that pencils, pens, ruler, and perhaps a calculator are readily at hand. The desk also provides a useful storage area for stationery and maybe a child's most treasured possessions. Paint or stain the desk to fit in with the scheme of the room in which it will be used, so that it becomes an attractive piece of furniture in its own right, as well as a very practical one. A stenciled pattern, perhaps featuring a traditional Pennsylvanian Dutch design, would make a particularly attractive decoration for a desk of this kind.

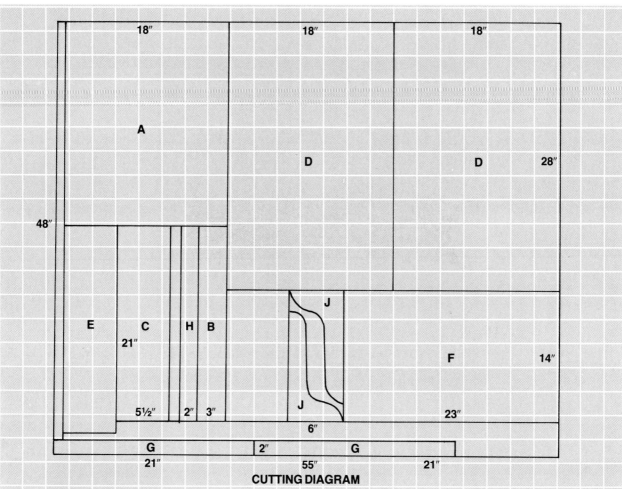

CUTTING DIAGRAM

Materials
- 48" x 55" of ½" plywood
- 20" of brass piano hinge and
- sufficient No.4 x ½" brass screws
- 30 No.6 x 1¼" brass screws
- 2 folding cupboard door stays with screws to fit
- small pack of finishing nails

Tools
- Panel saw
- jigsaw or coping saw
- power drill or brace
- screwdriver
- hammer
- plane and rasp
- homemade compass

Cutting instructions
all from ½" plywood
- bottom: 21" x 18" – A
- front: 21" x 3" – B
- back: 21" x 5½" – C
- sides: 18" x 28" sloping to 25½" (2) – D
- top: 23" x 6½" – E
- lid: 23" x 14" – F
- hinge reinforcements: 21" x 2" (2) – G
- cross brace for legs: 21" x 2" – H
- brackets 12" x 6" (2) – J

Construction
1. Taking one of the side pieces (D), select one 18" edge to be the top. From one corner, mark a point 2½" down the side. From the other corner, mark a point 5½" in, along the top. Join these two points, and cut off the waste with a saw, thus forming the slope for the desk top.

2. From the bottom edge, measure up 8" on one side. Using a compass, set a 4" radius and draw a half circle. Repeat at a point 17" up, and then draw a connecting line between the top edges of each circle. Cut, and remove the drawn piece to give the side shape. Repeat for the other edge. In a similar manner, on the bottom edge, mark points at 6" in from the corners. With the compass set at 2" radius, draw in the same shape. Cut out as above.

3. Repeat (1) and (2) for second side.

4. Take the desk bottom (A) and mark out a line at ¼" from both 21" edges. This is the center line for screw holes. Drill and countersink holes for three No.6 screws. Now screw through these to the front (B), lapping the bottom over the front and gluing

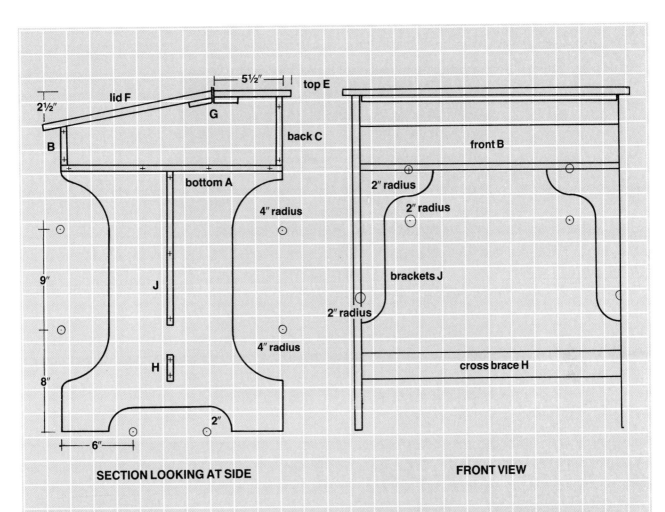

SECTION LOOKING AT SIDE

FRONT VIEW

for a firm fit. Join the desk back (C) in the same way.

5. Draw a horizontal line at 22¼" from the bottom edge of each side piece. Through this line, drill and countersink four holes for No.6 screws, through which the desk bottom will be fixed. Drill two holes in the front and back edges at the top of each side, through which pieces (B) and (C) will be attached. Screw and glue together, taking care that all edges at the top are flush.

6. The cross brace (H) and the two side brackets (J) can now be fitted after planing all edges smooth. The top of the brace (H) is at 6" from the bottom of the side (D) along the vertical center line. Drill and countersink two holes for No.6 screws in side (D) for fixing (H), and similarly three holes higher up the same line for fixing supports (J). Drill three further holes through the base of the desk to line up with the top of brackets (J). Screw and glue together.

7. The hinge reinforcements (G) can now be fitted to the 23" edge of the top (E) and the lid (F). These should be glued and nailed 1" in from the sides.

8. Now fasten the top to the desk, taking care that the hinge edge coincides with the points where the sides slope down for the lid. The top is fastened using two screws at each side (D), and three into back (C). The reinforced edge of lid (F) should now be planed to allow it to come flush with the top.

9. Fit the piano hinge to the lid and then to the top. It will be easier to remove the top from the desk first, and then to refasten when the hinge has been fixed.

10. Fit the cupboard door stays between the lid and the sides.

11. Fill all holes, sand thoroughly, and finish either in stain and varnish or with paint. Decoration can be added using a stencil.

Hobby Horse

This is an excellent toy for run-about play and leaves a lot to a child's imagination. Paint or stain the horse in realistic or fantasy colors and perhaps add a woolen mane. The hobby horse is simple to make. Change the shape of the head and you could build a dinosaur, a camel, or an elephant in exactly the same way, providing your child with an alternative and entertaining means of make-believe transport and many happy hours of play.

Materials
- 20″ x 12″ of ⅜″ plywood, or 10″ x 12″ of ¾″ plywood
- 4′ of 1″ diameter dowel, or a broom handle
- 10″ of ¾″ diameter dowel
- 12″ of 1″ x 2″ softwood (actual size ¾″ x 1½″)

Tools
- electric jigsaw or coping saw
- rasp or surform plane
- electric drill or brace with 1″ and ¾″ bits

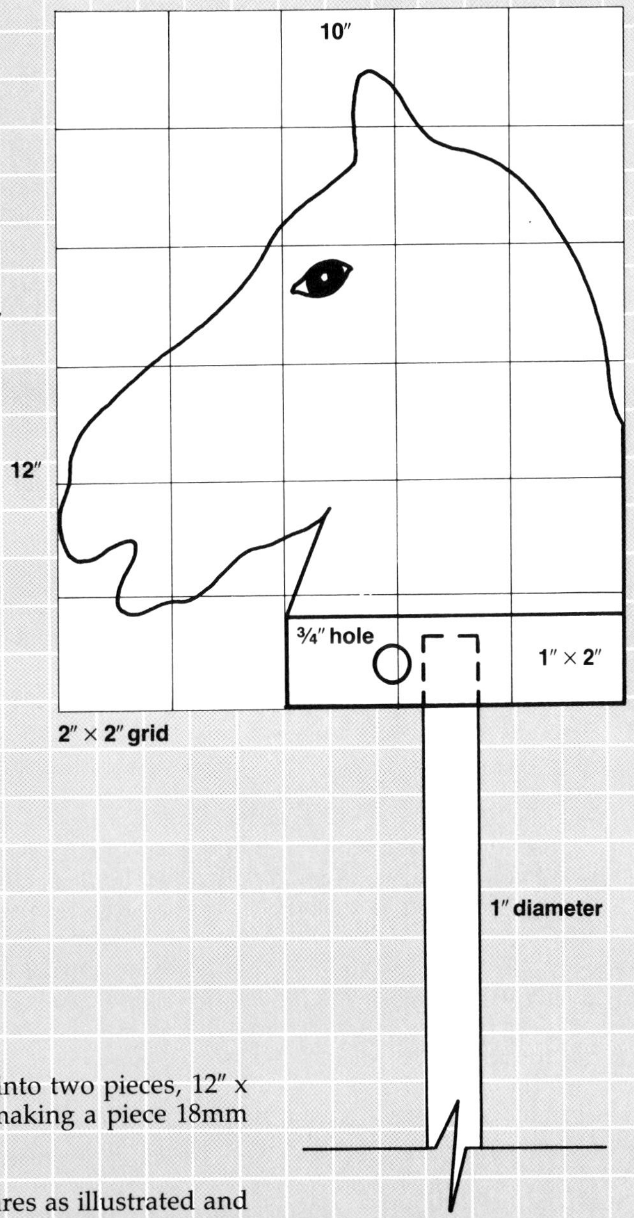

10″

12″

¾″ hole

1″ × 2″

2″ × 2″ grid

1″ diameter

Construction

1. If using ⅜″ plywood, cut into two pieces, 12″ x 10″, and glue back-to-back, making a piece 18mm thick. Leave until set dry.

2. Mark out a grid of 2″ squares as illustrated and draw in the head. (If desired, adapt to your own design.) Using the jigsaw, cut out the shape.

3. Cut two 6″ lengths of 1″ x 2″ softwood. Glue and nail these on both sides of the head at the neck to make the collar. When the glue has dried, shape the rough edges, and smooth the whole head with fine sandpaper.

4. On the underside and in the center of the ¾″ ply in the middle of the collar, drill a 1″ hole to a depth of 1¼″ to locate the handle. Don't use a flat bit as this will tend to split the wood. Instead, use a normal drill bit, and either clamp in a vise or get someone to hold the head steady so that the hole is drilled accurately.

5. At a point on the side of the collar and just to the front of the hole you have just drilled for the handle, drill a ¾″ hole through the collar. Cut a 10″ length of ¾″ dowel. After rounding off the ends with a surform and sandpaper, glue into place centrally in the ¾″ hole. Similarly, glue the 1″ dowel into position, cutting this to a length to suit the child, but bearing in mind that he or she will grow.

6. Drill a small hole through the back of the horse's head, and thread through a length of string or leather to make a bridle.

7. Finish as desired in stain or paint. Use an indelible felt-tip pen to draw in the eyes.

Pull-along Snakes

Children from eighteen months to three years will be fascinated by this pull-along snake. The characteristic wriggle is achieved by drilling the axle holes off-center. Paint or stain the snake's component parts in a variety of bright colors. Give the basic pull-along toy a differently shaped head and your child might have a tame crocodile to play with, too.

Materials
- 5′ of thick nylon cord, $\frac{3}{16}$″ diameter
- $7\frac{1}{2}$″ of $1\frac{7}{8}$″ diameter dowel
- $15\frac{5}{8}$″ of $\frac{7}{8}$″ x $\frac{7}{8}$″ hardwood
- $14\frac{1}{4}$″ of $\frac{3}{4}$″ diameter dowel
- $\frac{3}{4}$″ diameter wooden beads (16)
- $21\frac{1}{2}$″ of $\frac{1}{4}$″ nylon rod or dowel
- 1 large bead for head

Tools
- saw
- drill with $\frac{3}{16}$″, $\frac{1}{4}$″, and $\frac{5}{16}$″ bits

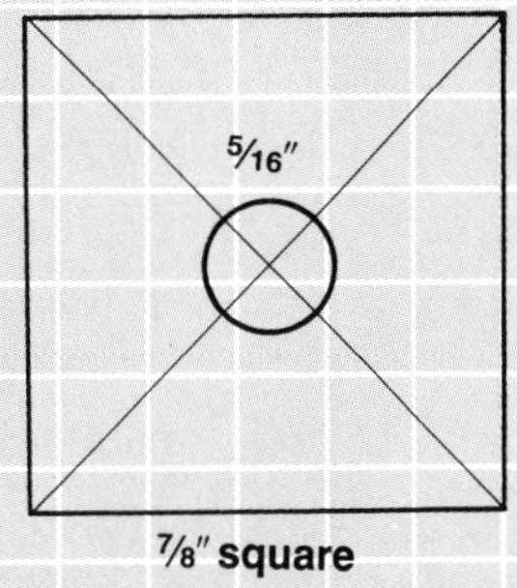

$\frac{5}{16}$″

$\frac{7}{8}$″ **square**

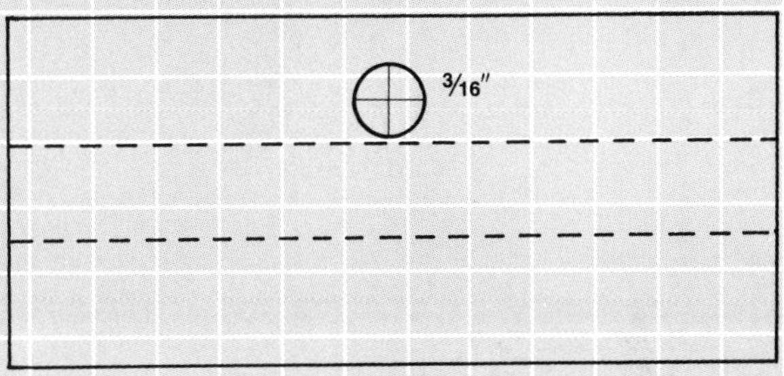

$\frac{3}{16}$″

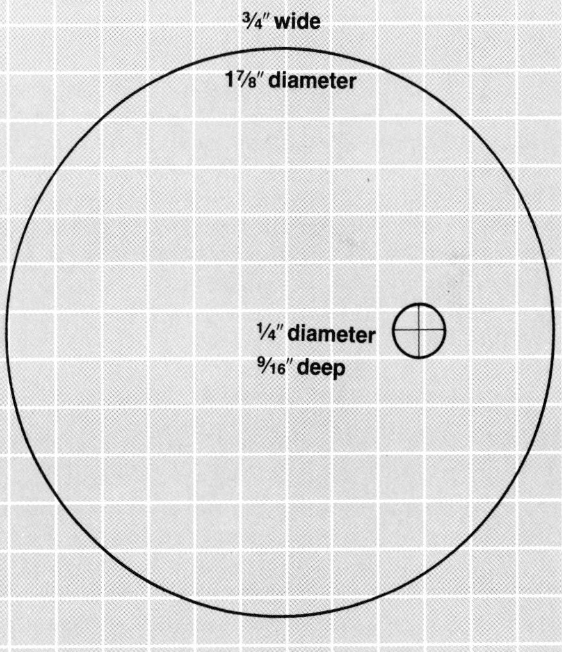

Construction

1. To make the wheels, cut $\frac{3}{4}$″ wide sections of $1\frac{7}{8}$″ diameter dowel. With a $\frac{1}{4}$″ bit, drill two with holes centrally and eight with holes offset from the center, $\frac{1}{4}$″ from the edge. All holes should be drilled to a depth of $\frac{9}{16}$″. (Note that special attachments can be purchased to stop the drill entering the wood beyond a pre-determined depth.)

2. To make the axle supports, cut five lengths of $\frac{7}{8}$″ x $\frac{7}{8}$″ hardwood. Drill through the center of each with a $\frac{5}{16}$″ bit. In the center of two sides, drill a $\frac{3}{16}$″ hole as shown in the diagram.

3. To make the body, cut twelve $1\frac{1}{8}$″ lengths of $\frac{3}{4}$″ diameter dowel. Drill a hole through the center of each using a $\frac{3}{16}$″ bit. At the same time, clear the hole in the beads with the same bit.

4. To make the axles, cut five lengths of $4\frac{1}{4}$″ from the $\frac{1}{4}$″ nylon rod.

5. To make the head, use a large macramé bead. Either paint in the eyes or use ring-binder reinforcers.

6. Assemble in alternating combinations, and adjust the offset wheels to give an undulating gait. The interspersed beads make the body flexible. The wheels work any way up, so that the toy will always follow along behind without your child having to stop to set it right.

$\frac{3}{4}$″ **wide**

$1\frac{7}{8}$″ **diameter**

$\frac{1}{4}$″ **diameter**
$\frac{9}{16}$″ **deep**

Toy Storage Chest

Comparatively few children have a playroom of their own where toys can be left around, so this well-designed storage chest will be particularly useful. Encourage your child to help with tidying away toys at the end of a day's play. Inside the chest are two handy trays for storing smaller toys. These lift out to reveal a larger storage area beneath. The lid hinges right over so that there should be no danger of it dropping down if you tell your child always to open it fully. The chest, since it is on casters, can be wheeled easily to wherever you would like to place it. Start to give such encouragement at an early age and tidiness could easily become a habit. Decorate the chest with a painted scene or a stenciled design, your child's name, letters of the alphabet, with a frieze, or leave it plain, either stained or painted in a bright color. Do be sure, as always, to warn your toddler about the dangers of using a chest like this as a hiding place.

Materials

- 4' x 6' of ⅜" plywood
- 1½" x 2½" of ⅛" plywood
- 16" of 1" x 2" softwood (actual size ¾" x 1½")
- 5' of ⅜" x 1¼" softwood stop
- 12" of ¾" quarter round
- approximately 60 No.4 x 1½" screws
- small pack of 1" brads
- small pack of 1½" brads
- set of 4 furniture casters
- 29" of 1" piano hinge, or ¾" crank hinges (3)

Tools

- saw
- jigsaw
- rasp plane
- drill
- screwdriver

Cutting instructions

from ⅜" plywood
- front and back: 27½" x 16½" (2) – A
- sides: 15¾" x 16½" (2) – B
- base: 27½" x 16½" – C
- lid: 29" x 17½" – D
- tray sides: 5½" x 15⅝" (4) – W
- tray ends: 3¾" x 11" (4) – X
- tray dividers: 1⅞" x 11" (2) – Y
- tray bases: 15⅝" x 11¾" (2) – Z

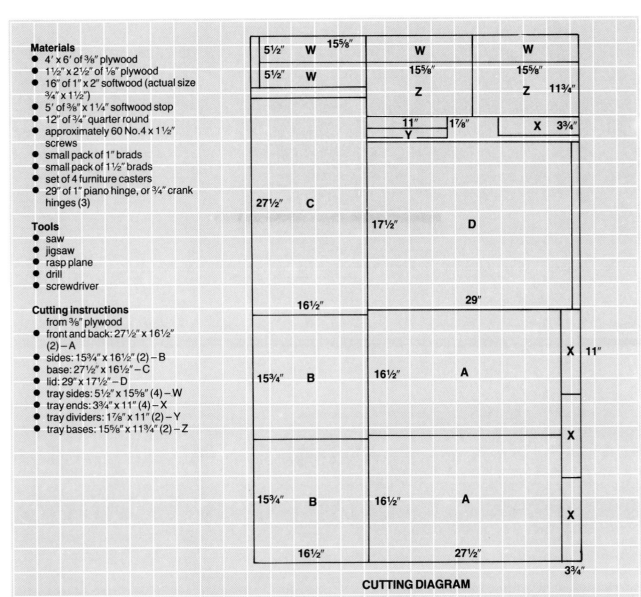

CUTTING DIAGRAM

Construction

1. In the shorter sides of (A), mark out and drill holes to clear a size 4 screw, ³⁄₁₆" from the edge, drilling four holes per side. In the same way, mark out the base (C) with holes at 4" intervals, all the way around.

2. Screw and glue pieces (A) and (B), and then fix the assembled unit to base (C).

3. Cut lengths of 1" x 2" softwood to reinforce the top and bottom of the box, and glue and nail into position as shown in the diagram.

4. Cut two lengths of ⅜" x 1¼" stop, and fix to the inside of pieces (A), so that the top edge is 6" from the top of the box. These will act as support for the trays.

5. Cut four pieces of ¾" quarter round, each 3" long and round off the top edge of each. Glue and press these into the four inside corners at the base. These are to take the casters.

6. When the glue has dried thoroughly, turn the box over and drill holes for the caster shanks at 1¼" from each side, at each corner. Bang in the caster shank and pop in the casters.

7. To strengthen the lid, glue and nail 1" x 2" softwood around the inside edges of the top. Round off with a plane, and sand smooth. ¾" piano hinges can be used to hold the lid in position, but crank hinges are preferable. These enable the lid to swing right around and parallel to the back, so that there is no risk of it dropping down unexpectedly.

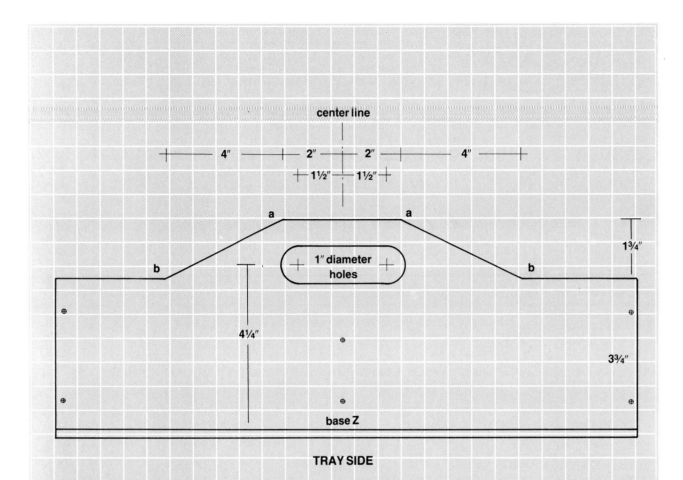

TRAY SIDE

Note that if piano hinges are to be used, it is essential to attach metal trunk stays to hold the lid in the vertical position.

8. The cutting list specifies enough pieces for two trays. If only one is required, use half the number of pieces.

9. Sides (W) have to be shaped in order to make handles as shown in the diagram. Draw a center line and measure 1½", 2", and 4" either side of this. Then, along each 1½" line at a distance of 4¼" up from the base line, mark two more points. These are the centers of holes for the handle cutouts. Using these points as a center, drill out two holes using a 1" bit. (To avoid the backs splintering when drilling holes, back up the piece with a scrap of plywood, and drill through both at same time.) Use a jigsaw to shape out the wood between the two circles.

10. Mark points *a* and *b* either side of the center line, *a* at 2" from the center line and 5½" from the base, *b* at 6" from the center line and 3¾" from the base. Join up and cut to shape.

11. Drill holes to clear No.4 screws and countersink. Drill two holes at ³⁄₁₆" from the edges and two on the center line for the tray divider. (Note that the divider is only 1⅞" deep.) Now glue the tray sides (W) to the ends (X). Drill and countersink the base (Z) and fix to the tray sides. Finally, fit the divider (Y) into place, glue, and screw.

12. Fill all countersunk holes with filler, sand smooth, and either paint or use stain and varnish.

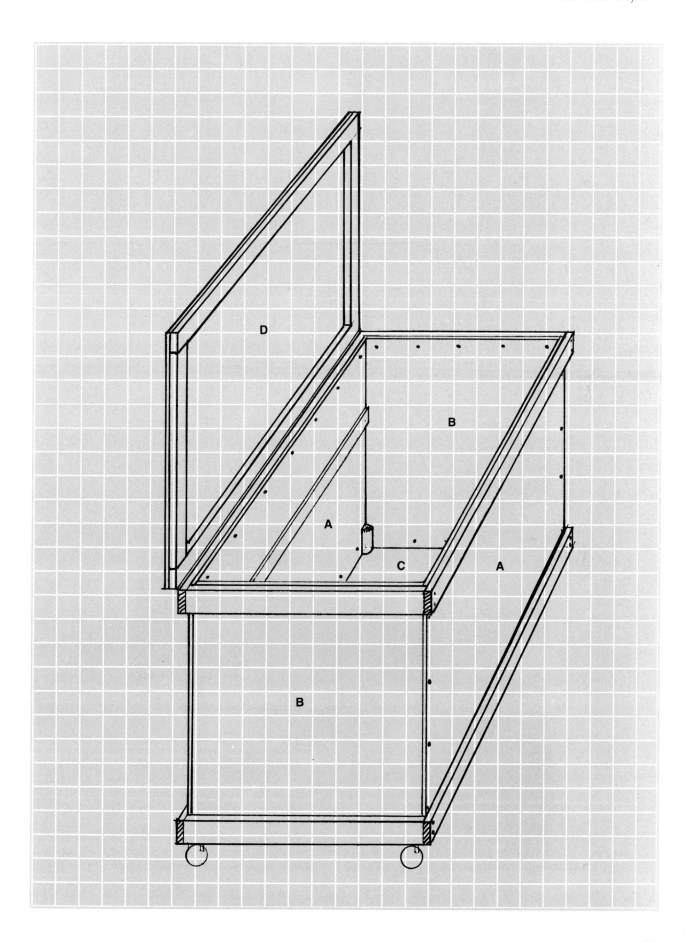

A Perfect Finish

The finish selected for any of the items made will be a matter of personal choice. There is today a much greater trend toward natural finishes with no heavy buildup of lacquers. But for some items—toys in particular—you will probably want to choose a gloss finish in a strong primary color.

Wood does not, of course, have to be finished at all, and in many countries much hardwood furniture is sold in an unfinished state. As long as any marks are removed with fine sandpaper or steel wool and the environment is dry, the piece should remain just as serviceable as if painted or stained.

Most people will, however, prefer to apply some sort of finish to enhance the appearance of the piece. This can be done in a variety of ways, with use of stain, lacquer, varnish, paint, shellac, oils, or wax. Each will have a very different effect, and your choice will depend not only on the look you wish to achieve, but also on the type of wood. But whatever finish you choose, it will be successful only if the surface has been correctly prepared.

Preparation

The first essential in preparing any surface is to get as even a finish as possible. Clear varnishes, in particular, will accentuate any scratches or marks. Careful cutting should help keep planing or sanding to a minimum.

Sanding

Sanding is by far the best method of getting a really smooth finish. There are various types of abrasive papers available, but the most commonly used is sandpaper. This will suffice for most jobs. The size of the particles of grit on the surface of the paper governs its roughness, and there are set standards for the various grades. Most people, however, buy papers by the more general terms of "coarse," "medium" or "fine."

When sanding, start with the finest sandpaper that is appropriate for the particular surface on which you are working. Birch plywood, for example, which has been used in most of the items featured, is quite smooth and will only therefore require rubbing with a fine paper. With a rougher, more open-grained wood, it is necessary to start with a very coarse grade. Always work from coarse through medium to fine. This will ensure the best finish possible.

Apart from the occasions when you are working on a very small area, we recommend that a sanding block be used. This can be made by wrapping the sandpaper around a flat wood block that will ensure that the whole of the paper is held flat against the surface. If a block is not used, and the sandpaper is simply held in the palm of the hand, it will only cut where it is pressed against the wood. It is often worth making a matching-shaped block out of cork if you have to smooth down a shaped edge or molding. To ensure that the block matches the molding exactly, cut it roughly to shape, place a piece of sandpaper on the molding, and rub the block to shape on it.

After sanding, remove any grit and dust from the surface with a fine brush, making strokes in the direction of the grain. This will ensure that all crevices are cleared. For a really smooth surface, wipe over with a damp cloth to raise the grain slightly. Allow the wood to dry, and then sand again with a very fine sandpaper.

If the sandpaper becomes clogged during use, clean it by running the back over the edge of the work bench or table. Remember, too, that sandpaper must be stored in a warm, dry place, as it is useless when damp. Similarly, do not try to use sandpaper on damp wood as it will never produce a good finish.

Power orbital sanders can be extremely useful, and save a lot of time, but they require experience to obtain the best effect, especially on veneers. If you are using a power sander, take care to examine the surface periodically by eye and also by touch. Always finish off by hand, working along the grain.

Patching and filling

Conceal any deep scratches or small holes in the surface with wood filler. Fillers can be purchased in a variety of shades, but it should be noted that they will rarely match the wood perfectly and may even have the effect of highlighting the mark rather than hiding it. Great care is therefore needed.

Where the work is to be painted or stained, filling will be easier as the finish will mask any filler. Where no paint or stain is to be used and a perfect color match is desired, a homemade filler can be made by mixing sawdust from the wood to be filled with a small amount of woodworking glue. Make this into a paste and fill the hole or scratch mark immediately. Sand it smooth when dry.

Staining

While most woods look very good when left in their natural color, staining can also produce a fine appearance particularly when one of the more attractive shades of stain is used. If a particular shade is desired, stains of the same type and of the same manufacture can be mixed. Make sure, however, that you mix sufficient to complete the whole job as it is extremely difficult to mix two batches and achieve an identical shade. Care must also be taken to avoid spilling drops of stain on any untreated areas as these will soak in and show as dark patches.

Stains are either oil- or water-based. If in doubt, use the latter as they are much easier to work with and should not cause any chemical reaction. However, the wood will require sanding after application of the stain, as water stains raise the grain. Before staining the main piece, take a scrap piece of the same lumber and experiment with the stain. Allow the first coat to dry, and then apply a finishing coat.

Using a non-fluffy cloth or a brush, apply a coat liberally over the whole of the surface, working in the direction of the grain. Before the stain has dried, wipe off the excess with a clean, dry cloth in order to get an even tone. If an uneven final coloring is to be avoided, care should be taken when working on a large area that drying out does not occur before the whole surface has been covered with stain. Remember, too, that it is always better to put on two or three diluted coats of stain rather than one heavy coat that may end up looking blotchy.

Unlike water-based stains, oil-based stains dry slowly so that there is plenty of time to work in the color. They do not raise the grain and therefore do not require sanding as do water-based stains. Apply the stain with a cloth in the same way as for a water-based stain, and even out the color while the stain is still wet. Do not use an oil-based stain where a lacquered finish is to be applied as the two will react.

Grain filling

Today, the trend is to leave wood looking as natural as possible, so that the texture of the grain can be felt and seen. Grain fillers are therefore usually unnecessary. However, for a really glossy finish, the wood surface must be very smooth and a grain filler will be required. This is particularly so in the case of coarse-grained woods like oak, ash, or mahogany that have fairly rough surfaces even after sanding.

Fillers can be purchased in the form of either liquid or paste and to match the type of finish you will be using, whether oil or lacquer.

Rub the filler into the grain using a stiff brush. Then remove it from the surface with a rough cloth before it has dried completely so that the pores are filled, but no filler is left on the surface of the grain. When it is thoroughly hard and dry, sand lightly in the direction of the grain. As with staining, it is better to test the filler on a scrap before applying to the final piece.

Linseed oil

Linseed oil is the cheapest of the oil finishes and is available raw or boiled, the latter drying more quickly. It gives an extremely pleasing finish, but has the disadvantage that it requires many coats and is not particularly resistant to heat.

However, in common with other oil finishes, linseed oil is easy to use and needs no special preparation of the wood. It should be noted that it will darken the wood, giving a tough mat finish without covering up the grain and texture. The finish improves with age and is water-resistant. Resistance to marking and damage can be built up over the years by applying additional light coats of oil which should be rubbed in well.

Woods most suited to a linseed oil finish are teak, rosewood, and mahogany. Lighter colored woods, such as beech and sycamore, easily discolor, and softwoods, such as pine, are not really suited to oil finishes at all.

After preparing a mixture of one part linseed oil and one part turpentine, apply the mixture liberally across the grain, using either a cloth or a brush. After leaving for an hour or so, wipe the surface with a non-fluffy, dry cloth, and leave for at least a day before applying a second coat. Up to four applications of the mixture may be required for non-oily timbers. A good sheen can be built up by rubbing hard with a soft cloth. By using some wax polish, an even better finish will be produced.

Wax finish

Wax can be used either on top of a sealer or on bare wood. It will give a deep mat finish that is natural-looking and easily renewed.

Traditional wax polishes were prepared from a mixture of turpentine, beeswax, and carnauba wax. Modern polishes contain silicones and driers, which give a better resistance to marking and cut down the work of application. We recommend that you buy a good quality paste wax rather than using a spray or liquid.

Like oil finishes, wax has to be maintained and needs more careful treatment than a lacquered finish. Most woods can be waxed quite successfully, you will find.

Oak is particularly well suited to waxing, but softwoods and sycamore and ash will tend to look dirty after a while as the wax begins to work into the grain.

Apply the wax as a paste, thinning it with turpentine if necessary. Allow it to harden for about ten minutes after applying with a soft, non-fluffy cloth. Buff with a clean soft cloth to achieve a really fine sheen and apply further coats, buffing well in between to produce a really beautiful finish. In order to make the wood more resistant to marks, finish first with a thin sealer coat of lacquer before applying the layers of wax.

Varnish and shellac finishes

Varnishing is the traditional technique for producing a clear finish, although it is often used with pigments for staining. Its use has largely been replaced by modern synthetic lacquers such as polyurethane, which dry more quickly and are far more water- and stain-resistant.

Shellac is another traditional finishing material that has always been popular because of its quick drying quality and because it is easy to apply. It has another very important quality in that it penetrates into the wood and therefore creates a much deeper hue than varnish or synthetic lacquers, but it does, of course, require a good wax coating to produce a hard-wearing finish.

Lacquers

For resistance to staining, heat, and general wear, modern synthetic lacquers such as polyurethane are unrivaled. They are ideal for the surfaces of children's furniture that will have to withstand a lot of knocks. They are also easy to apply. Most important, they are nontoxic.

The very best lacquered finish is obtained by spraying. Unless a great deal of painting is envisaged, it is unlikely that it will be worth investing in a spray gun, although these can often be rented. Most home craftsmen feel much happier using a brush and will achieve a perfectly satisfactory finish by this means. An extremely durable and smooth finish will be produced by first applying a sealing coat of thinned-down lacquer. When this is completely dry, rub down with very find sandpaper before applying the first full coat. Rub down again, then apply a second coat of lacquer.

Warning

The reader's attention is drawn to the fact that many modern lacquers and varnishes are not considered suitable for children's toys or equipment where the lead content is higher than ·25 percent. If at all in doubt, check with the store or the manufacturer before purchasing.

Stencils

Certain items of children's furniture lend themselves well to decoration with use of a stencil, and a wide variety of stencil designs—featuring animals, flora, or patterns based on traditional Pennsylvanian Dutch folk art, for instance—can be bought in book or loose form. Be sure to follow the instructions provided with the stencil exactly in order to achieve the desired result.

In particular, care will be needed to ensure that the stencil selected is of suitable size for the piece to be decorated. Take great care, too, with the cutting out of the design, particularly where it is intricate, so that there are no rough or jagged edges. Cut out only the solid areas of the design, and do so on a suitable surface such as wood, smooth-edged plate glass, or old newspaper.

Paint used for stenciling should be mixed so that it is quite thick, and a special stencil brush should be used. Keep a fresh brush for each color in the design, and paint with it held at right-angles to the area being worked, using a stippling motion, rather than painting with strokes.

It is essential to use masking tape in order to hold the stencil in position. Test the extent to which the paint is held on the brush on rough paper before to increase the durability of the design which you have produced in this way.

Some oiled stencils can be used again and even reversed. It is, however, essential thoroughly to remove any paint on the other side before doing so. Finally, you may wish to varnish the surface in order to increase the durability of the design.

Painting tips

To stop dust settling

If you are painting an item of furniture outdoors, in order to prevent any dust settling on the wet paint, sprinkle some water on the ground around the object you are painting.

Brushes

Before using a new brush, soak it in linseed oil for a day or so to soften the bristles. It is also usually best to use the new brush for an undercoat first of all, just in case there are loose bristles.

If you store a paint brush over night in water, you will need to dry it before use. Wrapping it tightly either in foil or in polythene is preferable.

When storing pots of paint

In order to prevent a skin forming on top of previously opened pots of paint, it is a good idea to ensure that you store them upside-down when you put them away.

When painting with a spray

Always wear a mask when working with a paint spray. The mask should cover both your nose and your mouth.

If you have a paint-stained cloth

Do not store an oil or paint-stained cloth. It is sometimes possible for spontaneous combustion to occur.

When using paint stripper

If you are using paint stripper, always see that you wear gloves. Be sure always to keep such chemicals well away from the reach of children, too; and never use paint stripper near a flame for fear of fire.

Index

absentee father 45
accidents 42-45
adoption 8-9
attachment, of child to
    babysitter 9-10
attention, plea for 26

bedtime 17-18, 30
behavior problems 21-22,
    26, 28
    sexual patterns of 16-17
bereavement, *see* death
bird feeder (construction
    project) 74-76
birthday parties 38-41
bit brace drill, *see* drills
bites 43
blisters 43
bonding, *see* attachment
bookends (construction
    project) 77-78
brace, *see* drills
bricks, *see* building blocks
bruises 43
building blocks
    (construction project)
    69-70
burns 43
    see also sunburn

C-clamp 48
car sickness 10, 37
    travel by 37-38
chalkboard and easel
    (construction project)
    54-56
childminder, attachment to
    9-10
chilling 43
chisels 48
choking 24, 44
comics 19
cradle (construction project)
    51-53
criticism 13-14
custody 27-28
cuts 44

dark, fear of the 17-18
death, explanation of 12-13
desk (construction project)
    79-81
discipline 31-32
divorce 27-28, 45
dollhouse (construction
    project) 71-73
dolls, boys playing with 16
drills 48-49
drugs 29-30

dumb insolence 26

ears, objects in 44
easel, *see* chalkboard and
education, *see* school
electric shocks 44
eyes, objects in 44

facts of life, *see* sex
    education
family, position of child in
    20
father figure 23
fear, of the dark 17-18
filling (woodworking) 91
finishing techniques
    (woodworking) 91
first aid 24-25, 43-45
fractures 44
funeral, attendance of child
    at 13

games, for car travel 37-38
    for birthday parties 40-41
gimlet 48-49
grain filling (woodworking)
    92
grandparent, death of 12-13

hammer 49
Heimlich maneuvre 24-25
highchair (construction
    project) 57-61
hobby horse (construction
    project) 82-83
horror stories 19, 20

incentives 13-14

job, *see* work

lacquers 93
lead content in paints and
    varnishes, warning 93
linseed oil (wood treatment)
    92
literature 19, 20
Lorenz, Konrad 9

make-up 27
'middle' child 20
miter box 49
money, spending 23-24, 37
mother, working 9-10

nails and screws 50
names, choice of 30-31
nose, objects in 44
nosebleeds 44

objects in ears, eyes, nose 44
only child 24
outings 36

painting tips 93
parents, children's
    emotions towards 26
patching (woodworking) 91
paternity leave 25
peanuts 25
plane (woodworking) 49
play 16
power drill, *see* drills
poisoning 44
praise, importance of 26-27
preparation (woodworking)
    91
promises, importance of
    keeping 33
pull-along toy (construction
    project) 84-85
punishment, *see* discipline

reading 19, 20
rewards 13-14
rivalry, sibling 22
rocking horse (construction
    project) 62-65
routine, importance of 30

safety, in the home 42-43
sanding (woodworking) 91
saw, coping 49
    dovetail 49
    hand 49
    jigsaw 49
    metal 49
school 13-14, 15-16, 21-22, 32
    see also teacher
screwdrivers 49
separation 45
    see also divorce
sex education 11-12
shellac finish
    (woodworking) 92-93
shock 44
shopping, with children 37
speech 22-23
splinters 44
sprains 44
squares (woodworking) 49
staining (woodworking) 92
stencils 93
stings 44
storage chest (construction
    project) 86-90
sunburn 45
surform plane, *see* plane
swimming 17

teacher, importance of
    meeting with 21-22, 33
temper tantrums 28
temperature, how to take
    child's 8
threats 31-32,
thumb-sucking 19
time, child's sense of 28-29
tools 48-49
toy chest, *see* storage chest
toys 16

unconsciousness 45

vacations 25, 27
vaccination, for whooping
    cough 24
varnishing (woodworking)
    91, 92
violence in literature, effect
    of 19, 20

wax finishing
    (woodworking) 92
weekend activities 36-43
wheelbarrow (construction
    project) 66-68
whooping cough,
    vaccination for 24
woodworking tools 48-49
    tips 50
work, bench 48
    during school vacation
    25-26
    see also mother, working

Further reading

*Earth Father, Sky Father: The
Changing Concept of Fathering*
by Arthur and Libby Colman
(Prentice-Hall, 1981).
Father: The Figure and the Force
by Christopher P. Anderson
(Warner,Books, 1983).
The Father's Almanac by S.
Adams Sullivan
(Doubleday, 1980).
*How to Deal with Your Acting Up
Teenager: Practical Self-Help for
Desperate Parents* by Robert and
Jean Bayard
(Accord Press, 1983).
How to Discipline with Love by
Fitzhugh Dodson
(Signet, 1978).
How to Father by Fitzhugh
Dodson (Signet, 1975).
*Raising Brothers and Sisters
Without Raising the Roof* by
Carole and Andrew Calladine
(Winston Press, 1983).
*Single Parenting: A Practical
Resource Guide* by Stephen L.
Atlas (Prentice-Hall, 1981).
*Talking with Your Child about
Sex: Questions and Answers for
Children from Birth to Puberty* by
Mary S. Calderone and James
Ramey (Ballantine, 1984).
Carpentry for Children by Lester
Walker (Overlook Press, 1982).
*The Complete Book of Home
Workshop Tools* by Robert
Scharff (McGraw-Hill, 1979).
Woodworking with Kids by
Richard Starr
(The Taunton Press, 1982)
*101 Ways to be a Long-Distance
Super-Dad* by George Newman
(Blossom Valley Press, 1981).

Useful addresses

**U.S. Consumer Product Safety
Commission**
Washington, DC 20207
(800) 638-8326

For the number of your local
Poison Control Center:
**National Poison Center
Network**
125 DeSoto St.
Pittsburgh, PA 15213
(412) 681-6669

**Big Brothers/Big Sisters of
America**
117 So. 17th St., Suite 1200
Philadelphia, PA 19101

**Parents Without Partners,
International**
7910 Woodmont Ave.
Bethesda, MD 20814
(202) 654-8850

**The Step Family Foundation of
America**
333 West End Ave.
New York, NY 10023
(212) 877-3244

Toughlove (an organization for
parents troubled by teenage
behavior)
P.O. Box 70
Sellersville, PA 18960
(215) 257-0421